Oceans

of

Blessings

by

Sister Agnes Holmes

Oceans of Blessings

Oceans of blessings, rivers of peace,
Streams of pure water falling at my feet.
Enjoying His presence every step I take,
Resting in His shadow in the heat of the day.

I am so happy! I found the pearl of great price.
I just started living when I surrendered my life.
I asked the Master, "Where do you feed your sheep?"
"Down by the shepherd's tent," He answered so sweet.

Into the holiest of holies, in the cleft of the rock,
I found myself hiding from the storms of the night
Listening for His voice, soon to say,
"The harvest is ended, my love, come away."

by Sister Agnes Holmes

Acknowledgements

With sincere heartfelt thanks to everyone that encouraged me and supported me to take on the task of writing a book sharing my experiences with the Lord. I want to say a special thank-you to my son, Bro. Joel Holmes, who encouraged me from the beginning to write a book. I would also like to thank my daughters, Juanita and Faith, for the countless hours of helping me gather and remember names, dates, and pictures and then putting it all together in the order that it should read. Thanks to Andrea, my granddaughter, taking time to locate pictures that were stored in various places. A very special thanks to Sister Betty Ollis for the numerous times of proofing, editing, and typing that she did regarding my book. Thank you also for the title *Oceans of Blessings*.

I want to express special thanks to Sister Jill Copeland who typed many pages with a word processor when the book was first being born. Many thanks to Sister Karen Holmes and Sister Margaret Echols for taking on the burden of re-typing my work at different time intervals when it had been laid on the shelf of time. Thank you Sister Georgia Best. You have stayed with this task from the start until it was a finished accomplishment.

I pray *Oceans of Blessings* will be a testimony to the glory of God, and that it will be an inspiration to each one who reads it.

Table of Contents

Page

Rock Front Church built in 1949

Church at Second and Buckeye that burned

Fifty-second Place Church

Past and Present Churches at 1401 Calvary, North Little Rock, AR

Foreword

Each of us is on a journey through life. In all our hearts, there are memories which have left their mark on our lives.

I was privileged to receive such a beautiful and rich Christian heritage. Dedicated, Holy Ghost-filled members of my family had already impacted my life by the time I received the Holy Ghost and was baptized in the lovely name of Jesus when I was only ten years old. And since that time, there have been so many victories, so many blessings, so many beautiful experiences that I have a great desire to share them with my children, my grandchildren, my great-grandchildren, my great-great-grandchildren, and my precious friends.

Throughout the years of my ministry, often when I would be preaching, the Holy Ghost would anoint me to tell some of my experiences. It seems so many times the Lord would use my humble, little stories to encourage and bless the people of God or to touch the hearts of the lost that they would be saved. Now, it is the desire of my heart that this book will bring glory to God and bless His people. I would like for all to share my testimony: "Every day with Jesus is sweeter than the day before."

Sister Agnes Holmes
January 2003

Chapter 1

My Grandparents

In the beautiful hills of Mississippi on a cold November day, a small fire burned in the fireplace. The fire was mostly coal because an old iron Dutch oven sat on the hearth with a few coals under it and fewer on top of the lid. Baking inside the oven was a cake. The ingredients had carefully been mixed in a large crock bowl and then beaten by hand several minutes before being poured into the Dutch oven. It was a wedding cake baked by the bride-to-be herself, for tomorrow was the wedding day of Melissa Bell, Mr. and Mrs. Porter's daughter, and George Holland.

Melissa's parents had known things were getting more serious between the young couple when George's visits became more frequent. Many Sunday afternoons they would hear the sound of the hoofs of George's beautiful red saddle horse down the gravel road. Soon George would be off the horse tying the reins to the hitching post. Over six feet tall with broad shoulders, blue eyes and black hair, he made a striking appearance as he greeted Melissa with a big smile.

Frequently they spent the afternoons sitting in the living room. In one room was an old pump organ, which George played as they sang gospel songs such as, "In a Land Where We'll Never Grow Old" and "Nearer My God to Thee."

Sometimes on Sunday afternoons when they got permission from Melissa's mother, they would go horseback riding. Melissa had her own saddle horse. Since she was only five feet three inches tall, she always looked so dainty sitting on the sidesaddle designed especially for ladies. Her long, full, ruffled skirt draping the large horse, she made a pretty picture with her lovely dark complexion, dark piercing eyes, and long lustrous black hair.

Mrs. Porter would stand in the doorway and watch George carefully

1

hold Melissa's arm as she mounted her horse. Handing her the reins, he would leap into his saddle. As they waved to her mother, they would hear her say the same words each time, "Be sure to be home before night."

Today was different; Melissa wouldn't see her husband-to-be. She was very busy pressing her clothes with the old fire irons that were heated by the same fire that was baking the wedding cake. The tantalizing aroma of the cake, filled with fresh homemade butter and Watkin's vanilla flavoring, permeated the entire house. As the cake browned and rose, it pushed the lid up slightly. Melissa's younger brothers and sisters could hardly wait until the next day when the cake would be cut.

It was just a small wedding — some aunts and uncles, cousins and neighbors. The Baptist pastor performed the simple ceremony. The wedding was small but the spirit of joy was great.

Soon the couple settled down on a little farm of their own as happy as any couple could be. About a year later, the couple was blessed with a beautiful baby girl whom they named Adelia. Two years passed and then came a bouncing baby boy, Willie. When Willie was two, his brother Charlie was born. Then two years later, October 16, 1893, the home was blessed again, this time with a beautiful baby girl, whom they named Ida Revella, my mother.

The family grew to six boys and four girls: Adelia, Willie, Charlie, Ida, Wiley, Monroe, Mynervia, Hiram, Matt, and Annie Bell. Mom said that when Grandma was expecting a baby she always wore full Mother Hubbard dresses disguising the fact. When a little newcomer was on the way, Grandpa would ask the children if they would like to go over to one of their aunts and spend the night. Since they all usually had to get up early and work hard, they were delighted with the break. They never dreamed that when Grandpa brought them home in the wagon the next morning, they would find a new little one lying in bed with their mother.

My grandparents were concerned with their children's spiritual training. Each Sunday morning, they loaded everyone into the wagon and rode a couple of miles to a little country Baptist church. The

My Aunts and Uncles
(L to R): Aunt Annie Bell, Uncle Matt Holland,
Uncle Monroe Holland, Uncle Wiley Holland, my
mother Ida Clark, Uncle Charley, Aunt Mynervia

2

ten children and their parents pretty well filled the wagon, and when they got to church they filled more than one pew.

My mother told me that families used to go and spend the night with friends and relatives. She remembered once when they were all loaded in the wagon on the way to spend the night with some of their folks, as they passed a house, the man came out, rang the dinner bell and said, "Hollands have swarmed and are settling over at Mr. Temple's." Mother said that it hurt her mother's feelings.

I remember when I was a little girl going with my grandmother and aunt to the little Baptist church. This would usually be when they had what they called protracted meeting. That was around July when the crops were already harvested. Services would convene day and night for a week. Long tables were set up under the trees outside the church. Linen tablecloths, which had been stiffly starched and ironed, were spread on the tables. All the ladies brought food each day. They cut the cakes and pies in pieces and placed them all over the table. Those pieces of pie (egg custard and all kinds) looked like a picture. There were dishpans of chicken pie with golden brown crust. These events would be about the only time I had a desire to go with my grandparents to church.

My grandfather was as honest as could be; in fact, he couldn't stand people who would lie, cheat, or steal. I remember my mother telling about a time after all the children except the youngest daughter, Annie Bell, were gone from home that Grandpa missed corn from the crib. He discovered a board pulled off on the back of a hole in the pile of corn where someone was coming at night and stealing it. He got a big steel trap and set it in this hole. About nine o'clock that night, they heard some one yelling for dear life. Grandpa shouted, "Annie Bell! Get up and light the lantern. We have someone in the trap!" Sure enough, his hand caught in the trap, was a man who lived nearby. Grandpa got inside the crib, opened the trap, and let the man pull his hand out.

One summer, boys were stealing Grandpa's watermelons, bursting and wasting them in the field. One day as Aunt Annie Bell was leaving for town, Grandpa exclaimed, "Annie Bell, I want you to go to Dr. Mullin's office and tell him to send some ipecac and a hypodermic syringe. I'm going to stop some boys from ruining my watermelon patch." That evening he went to the field and injected the ipecac in some of the largest melons in the patch.

Sure enough, that night the boys were hungry for watermelons. When they got to the field, they located the biggest ones, loaded them into their car and went home. After they ate the melons, they became so nauseated that they thought they would die. Someone was sent to Bude for Dr. Mullins.

The next morning when my grandfather started to the barn that was across the road from his house, Dr. Mullins drove up in his buggy on his way back to town. He drawled, "Mr. Holland, when I got there before daylight this morning, those boys were lying on the lawn, sick as could be." He continued, "Even the mother had eaten some. I felt sorry for the old lady and I fixed her a little stronger medicine than I did the boys."

My grandfather broke up watermelon and corn stealing. He was generous-hearted and would have given corn to the man or watermelons to the boys if they had asked, but he couldn't stand a thief.

Years ago my aunt came to visit me, bringing that old hypodermic needle, which she gave to Vaiden, my grandson. It must be over a hundred years old.

Aunt Annie Bell

Chapter 2

Mother

My mother didn't realize when she was growing up that just across the hills a couple of miles away in the home of Mr. and Mrs. William D. Clark, there lived the one with whom she would share her life. Ten years older than my mother, he was tall and handsome with black hair and beautiful deep blue eyes. Theirs was not a long courtship. The same hands that years before had baked the wedding cake in the fireplace in the old Dutch oven, now baked a wedding cake on a big wood stove. That day Mr. and Mrs. George Holland gave their daughter in marriage to my father, Mr. Byrd Clark.

On the twenty acres of land which my mother's parents had provided for them, they built a small house with a tin roof. They lived happily in this little house for many years.

When my daddy and mother married, my dad belonged to what was known as The Gospel Trumpet Church, a group of people that believed in sanctification. My mother was a Sunday school teacher in the Baptist church. Mother had been taught by her pastor that it was a shame for a woman to pray in public. When Daddy would get on his knees and pray at night, Mother would find a book to read or look at the Sears & Roebuck catalogue.

Their first baby was a boy named Clymouth. When he was three years old, another son, Pernell, was born. After Mother's second little boy was born, her health began to fail. One morning she awakened with a terrible pain in her side. Daddy called the doctor who diagnosed appendicitis and rushed her to the hospital in Natchez. When the doctor operated, it was found that her appendix had ruptured and infection had set up. For the next few days, Mother was very ill. The doctor found she had some more serious things wrong with her and needed another operation before she left the hospital. With this decision weighing heavily upon her mind, she went to sleep troubled, thinking of her young husband and two small sons and the present busy time on the farm. During the night, she dreamed her father was chastening her. When she awoke from this troublesome dream, she pondered what this could mean. Something seemed to say, "It's not your natural father, it's your Heavenly Father." When the doctor made his rounds that morning, she said, "Doctor, I want to go home. I'll come back later for the operation."

She left the hospital a very sick person. She rode the train back to Bude. When Daddy came in the buggy to meet her, he realized that Mother was much in need of the operation; she suffered much pain to ride the train and the ten-mile buggy ride home. She could never forget that day. She said, "It was less painful to walk than to ride."

As they were riding along on their way home, Daddy started telling her about something that was going on. She could tell he was bubbling inside; he was so excited. He said, "There's a big revival in progress every night in the school auditorium, conducted by Evangelist Jake Smith. The power of God is falling like rain and people are being slain under the power of God. Some are dancing, shouting, and speaking in tongues. The singing is so anointed and beautiful! The house is packed every night; I've never seen anything like it. The first time I visited, I just went to see, but it seems I just feel the Lord drawing me back every night. Regardless of how tired I am, I can't stay away."

My parents Ida and Byrd Clark

6

The next night Mother decided she would go and see. She was amazed; it was so different from any church she had ever attended. But there was something about it she liked. It was like the old song, " . . . and I went back again." It wasn't many nights before Daddy received the Holy Ghost with the evidence of speaking in tongues. In fact, numbers of people were being filled every night. Conviction fell on Mother and she went to the altar. After having prayed for the Holy Ghost a few nights, she got up from the altar one night after praying and saw Aunt Effie, Daddy's sister, still seeking. Mother went to her and started praying and the Holy Ghost fell on Mother. She started speaking in tongues and dancing in the Spirit. God instantly healed her body, allowing her to live to be eighty-one years old. She never did have to go back for the operation.

During this revival Mother's oldest sister, Aunt Adelia, and one of her brother's, Wiley, received the Holy Ghost. The revival lasted for weeks. Every night Daddy would leave the schoolhouse sometime around two or three a.m. to go home and get a nap so he could work in the field. Mother and Daddy said that many mornings there would be people passing their house after daylight walking home from the revival.

My daddy's parents became believers of this Gospel. My Grandmother Clark received the Holy Ghost and was baptized in Jesus' Name. Four of Daddy's sisters, Aunt Arie, Aunt Effie, Aunt Minnie, and Aunt Julie, also received the Holy Ghost.

After Mother received the Holy Ghost, she went to Grandma and said, "Mama, you know how sick I've been and how we have spent every dollar we had on doctor bills. The Lord has restored my health!"

One time when my two little brothers were visiting Grandmother's, Grandma was holding one of my aunt's little boys on her lap telling him, "You are Grandma's little man." My little brother, Pernell, spoke up and said, "Grandma, you know what I am?" Grandma asked "What, Son?" He said, "I'm a little Holy Roller." Clymouth, two years older, came home telling Mother what he said, and how embarrassed he had been.

Not long before I was born, my oldest brother, Clymouth, received the Holy Ghost. Mother told me how he would worship the Lord, shouting and rejoicing in the Spirit. Then the death angel visited our home. Clymouth became sick and with every kind of treatment the doctor gave him, he only grew worse. Daddy and Mother prayed and begged the Lord to heal him. It was mid-summer and the weather was hot. Clymouth was sitting in a rocking chair, burning with fever. Mother said they didn't have any ice. He looked up at my mother and said, "I wish it would rain." While Mother was standing by his chair, he noticed she was crying. He said, "Mama, don't cry. Just live for Jesus, shout the victory, and meet me." Before the sun set that evening, he went home to be with the Lord.

My Grandma and Grandfather Clark were still living on the eighty-acre farm where Daddy was raised. Even though there was a family cemetery three or four miles from there, Daddy decided he wanted him buried on the home place. Naturally, I don't remember him, but after I grew older, I would walk with my mother many times in the evening down to the little grave where my mother would weep and weep. Long boards lay on each side of the grave; there was no tombstone. Someone had made a little cross out of wood and I remember Mother painting it white and placing it at the head of his grave.

Later on, my grandfather passed away and we moved into the house with my grandmother because she was too old to live alone. Times were very hard and the eighty acres and home were sold for taxes. We moved away and someone else bought the place. Trees grew up and the little white cross and boards rotted and the little grave could no longer be found. But one day, on that first resurrection morning, that lost grave will be found. The ground will burst open and he will arise to meet the Lord in the air.

Nine days before Mother was expecting her third child, as she stood before the stove cooking breakfast, she heard a voice over her head call the name *Agnes*. Three days later as she stood in the same place, she had the same experience. Three more days passed and again the experience was repeated. When Mother mentioned this to her sister-in-law, who had received the Holy Ghost about the same time that she and my daddy had, she suggested, "Ida, maybe God is going to give you a baby girl and wants you to name her Agnes." And that's how I came to be named Agnes.

When I was two-and-a-half years old, our home was blessed with another baby boy. Mother named him Bernette. When I was seven years old, God gave me a little baby sister that brought lots of sunshine and joy and made us very happy. The first time I saw her, she looked like a doll with big beautiful blue eyes lying there by Mother. I picked up one of her little hands and said, "Mother, she is going to be a little grandmother because the palm of her little hand is wrinkled." I remembered Grandma Clark's hands looked that way.

Times were hard but it didn't keep us from being happy. Bernette and I enjoyed many hours playing together and building playhouses. We didn't have many toys bought from the store. A stick with a string tied on the end would be our horse and a stick with a forked end and a lid to roll would be our cars. I remember a playhouse that we built between the house and barn using boards that were used back in those days to roof houses. We would take those boards and make furniture like a couch, chairs, and victrola.

Bernette loved to sing in the playhouse. We would stack those boards and find a crooked stick that resembled the piece that held the needle on a victrola. Bernette would get inside and I would pretend that I put a record on, starting the victrola. Bernette would be inside the box singing.

In the afternoons, my mother would be a short distance away in the barn milking the cows. She would be in the Spirit, praying and speaking in tongues. One afternoon as she returned from milking, she stopped to hear Bernette sing. He couldn't see Mother, and I thought it was so funny. He was singing, "Hannah, why don't you open the door?" One verse used a little byword. He sang gleefully, "Hannah, why don't you open the _____ door?" My tune soon changed because Mother broke a switch using it on both of us. She raised us to love and fear the Lord.

My daddy's family was a lot different from my mother's family. Daddy had eleven brothers and sisters. They had a nice home with plenty of room, and were blessed with more material things than were Mother's family. I loved them dearly, but they always wanted everything quiet, and they went to bed by dark.

I loved it better at the Holland's. They cooked supper late, milked most of the time after dark, made molasses candy at ten o'clock at night, parched peanuts, and you could throw the hulls on the hearth. It was always noisy with laughter and talking.

When I was ten years old, an evangelist named Brother P. B. Showers came to our church to preach a revival. I got under conviction and began seeking the Holy Ghost. I went to the altar every service and prayed. When the revival closed, I still hadn't received the Holy Ghost, but one night a few weeks later, I received the Holy Ghost at home.

During this revival, Mother's brothers, Uncle Charlie, Uncle Hiram, Uncle Monroe, Uncle Matt, and her youngest sister, Annie Bell, received the Holy Ghost and were baptized in Jesus' name. Uncle Wiley was already preaching at the time of this revival. Uncle Matt and Uncle Hiram also received their call to preach.

Grandma Holland really grieved when the rest of her children became Pentecostal; however, Mother's parents did a good job raising them. Not one of their children ever had the habit of smoking or drinking, however, it takes more than good works. The Bible says, "We must be born of the water and the Spirit to make Heaven."

When I was young, the Lord would reveal things to me that were coming to pass. Sometimes when people were very sick, we would pray and the Lord would instantly heal them. Many times while praying for someone sick, while in the Spirit, I would see the form of an evil spirit that had them bound. I would scream and my Mother would encourage me not to be afraid but to keep praying until God rebuked the enemy. It seems that I felt the call to preach ever since I can remember. When I would be playing with other children, I loved to play church. I would say, "Let me be the preacher." Unknown to me, my mother would slip around and listen. Down from our house there was a blacksmith shop where farm tools were sharpened. There was a table at one end that was my platform. I remember I would feel the anointing so strong.

Mother and Uncle Wiley were called to preach. Mother, Daddy, Uncle Wiley and Aunt Eula began to work for the Lord together and held services in different communities. Their only means of travel was horse and buggy. Mother had a little folding pump organ that they would carry on the back of the buggy. She used to laugh and tell about their first street service that was held in the small town of Bude. Before the service started, Daddy suggested to Mother, Uncle Wiley, and Aunt Eula, "Let's try to hold it down and not be too demonstrative since this is our first service here." Uncle Wily and Aunt Eula were good singers; he sang lead and she sang alto. The service started with them singing and Mother playing the organ, and the presence of the Lord fell like rain. Daddy got to feeling the power of the Lord so strong and got so happy that he wrapped his arm around one of the posts that held up the roof and went round and round, shouting as loud as he could.

On one of these appointments to preach at McCall's Creek, they were driving their horse and buggies along together. They had to cross a creek where there wasn't a bridge. The creek was up, due to a big rain the night before. Uncle Wiley suggested that Aunt Eula get in the buggy with Mother and Daddy. He would drive his buggy across first and see if he could cross. The water was deep and swift. In the middle of the stream, the current turned the horse and buggy upside down. Before it flipped, Uncle Wily jumped out into the creek. The horse and buggy got straightened up and he made it safely across. Even though his suit was soaking wet, he told Daddy, Mother and Aunt Eula to go back home and he would go on to fulfill the appointment.

My parents Byrd and Ida Clark

Chapter 3

Childhood Memories

During my childhood and teenage years, it was common when friends and neighbors visited one another for someone to make the suggestion, "Let's all seek the Lord awhile." A spiritual environment such as this gave me some unforgettable memories.

When I was but a small child, some of my Mother's friends made a lasting impression upon my life. One friend that we visited often was Sister Womack, who really walked with God. On one of our visits in the cold winter, she was sitting by the fireplace suffering intense pain from a toothache. Her husband finally said, "I'll go hook the horse to the buggy and take you to Bude to the dentist." As she sat there praying, she begged, "Bill, just wait a few minutes. I'm asking God to pull this tooth." All at once that big jaw tooth fell into her hand and she showed it to her husband!

Later on that spring, Sister Womack was planting corn as W. H., her son, plowed, when another tooth began to ache. She sat down on the row and began praying. W. H. asked, "What's the matter, Mom?"

"I have a bad toothache," she replied, "but I know what the Lord did a few months ago." W. H. plowed on down the row, and when he came back, she was rejoicing, holding the tooth up. "Thank God! He has done it again!" she shouted.

After these two miracles Sister Womack experienced one even greater. Her husband suddenly became sick, falling across the bed and dying. She told W. H. to hurry and go get his brother who lived about two miles away. It didn't take W. H. long to return with his brother. When they walked into the room, they realized their dad had no breath or pulse. Sister Womack, who was praying, cried, "I believe God is going to bring him back."

The older son said, "Mom, he's gone. There's no sign of life. Let's call the funeral home."

"No, just wait," she persisted. After he had been dead for a couple of hours, Sister Womack laid her hands on his head, and God miraculously raised her husband from the dead! I think of the Scripture in which the Apostle Paul exclaimed, "Why should it be thought a thing incredible with you, that God should raise the dead?"

In our circle of friends was the family of Brother Jim and Sister Dora Howell, some of the most prayerful people we had ever seen. They were poor sharecroppers on Mr. Dillon's farm. It was a happy time for them when some Pentecostals started a revival nearby. The "church facilities" were simple: some seats were built, some lanterns hung. Sister Dora and their ten children attended each night, and as sure as Sister Dora got to church, she shouted and danced so much that the soles of her shoes wore out.

The custom at that time was for the landlord to make arrangements for the workers to buy their food and clothing before the harvest and then to settle the debt when the cotton crop was sold. Sister Dora asked Mr. Dillon about getting a new pair of shoes. Mr. Dillon, who did not believe the Pentecostal doctrine, scornfully replied, "No! I see you shouting every night, wearing your shoes out." Sister Dora never said a word. She just went back to church the next night and shouted some more.

Mr. Dillon decided not to attend church that night, but to stay home and rest. God sent an angel to his house. All night long he heard the sound of someone shouting and dancing in the attic above his bed. He was unable to sleep. Early the next morning, he knocked on the Howell's door.

House that the angel of the Lord shouted all night keeping Mr. Dillon awake.

13

"Mrs. Dora," he said, "I have come to take you to Tylertown to buy you a pair of shoes."

We have been in their home when Sister Dora would cook dinner or supper. It was in the 1930's; times were hard. She would take a five-cent can of salmon and make a big skillet of gravy. This was a special treat since most of the time the gravy was plain. The meal was completed by a big pan of biscuits. Twelve of them and five of us would sit at a long table with a bench on each side. Before being seated, we got down on our knees and prayed. The gravy and biscuits were passed around the table until around twenty people were filled, and gravy and biscuits were still left! I did not think anything of it at the time, but since then, I have realized that God had to miraculously multiply that food. The gravy bowl was a normal-size serving dish. Why should God not do this? He is the same God who kept the meal barrel and the cruse of oil from going empty in the widow's house when the Prophet Elijah was a guest there.

Times were really hard, but Holy Ghost-filled people were happy. Going to church was our chief joy. I recall walking six miles to church one night with the Howell family. Brother Howell had pink eye so badly that his son had to lead him twelve miles to and from church, but he couldn't bear the thought of missing church. I fear for folks today who look for any little excuse to miss going to the house of the Lord.

There was never a dull moment in our home. Daddy and Mother were real prayer warriors. Sick people came to be prayed for or my parents were called to go to their homes. There were times when the church would be without a pastor, and evangelists would come and stay in our home. One evening Brother and Sister Johnny McGhee came to preach and Mother prepared supper for them before service. While we were eating, Mother ran to milk the cows. I was almost seven years old and accidentally spilled my big glass of milk in the lap of Brother McGhee's blue serge suit. When I was grown and married, Brother McGhee still teased me about his blue serge suit, the only one he had at that time. He said the cleaners could never get the stain out.

Many times Bernette and I would be playing while my mother was cooking supper and Daddy was praying. I could never keep playing while hearing him pray. It would be dark and the only light was from coal oil lamps. I would go from room to room until I found him. There in the dark I would kneel down by him and pray as long as he prayed.

Prayer was an important part of our lives. Mother prayed while she was milking the cows, washing the clothes, sewing, and cooking. Many times when working in the field, we all knelt at the end of the row and had a prayer meeting.

Mother and her sister, Adelia, would take the horse and buggy, collecting food contributions. Sometimes they would stop at homes in the community and ask the residents if they would like to send a jar of fruit or something to Mr. and Mrs. Dickerson, who were very poor. Times were very different then; there weren't any relief programs or social security. Some of the neighbors would be glad to contribute and others would say, "No! Let their boys take care of them." I remember one time Aunt Effie, Dad's sister, made a beautiful quilt. To those of you who have never made a quilt, you have to piece the stars, put them together, make a lining, sew it into frames, lay the quilt top on the lining, then quilt for hours. After she had spent many days quilting and was taking it off the frames, the power of the Lord came on her. She began shouting and rolling the quilt up in her arms. The Holy Ghost revealed to her to take it to Mr. and Mrs. Dickerson. She did this without questioning the Lord, even after all her labor.

Daddy raised hogs and smoked and cured the meat in the smoke-house for winter. It was nearing spring when Mother told Daddy, "I feel in the Holy Ghost we need to take the Dickerson's a shoulder of meat." Daddy said, "You need to pray the Lord will move on somebody to bring us one because we are almost out." Mother said, "All right." A few days passed. One evening Mother and Dad looked outside and saw a big dog they had never seen before trotting off carrying the shoulder of meat. The smokehouse door had been left open accidentally. Daddy started chasing the dog. Mother said, "You won't catch him because that was Mr. Dickerson's meat." Daddy said, "I'll get the dog." They had one piece of meat left; he put poison in a piece and left it out, but the dog never came back. My Mother drilled in us children that we must fear the Lord and do our best to do His will.

While growing up, I was always impressed with the way that my Uncle Wiley, my mother's brother, was always singing or whistling what-ever work he was doing. One time he was led by the Holy Ghost to go to Brookhaven, Mississippi, and preach on the streets that Saturday. This was about twenty-seven miles away. He didn't mind walking; he was used to that, but this time he was on a fast. He was also used to fasting. I've known him to fast ten days in hot summer time and saw logs every day.

As he walked to Brookhaven that morning, he became so weak that he lay down on the side of the road to rest. While he was lying there, the Lord spoke to him to break the fast. He said, "Lord I don't have anything to eat." He got up and continued on his journey. When he had walked a little way, he found stalks of sugar cane lying in the road. He picked one up, peeled it, and began chewing it, enjoying the juice. Some time that morning some-one has been hauling cane to the syrup mill and had lost some along the way. The cane juice gave him strength to make the journey.

As he preached on the street that day, two brothers were convicted. God saved them, and later called them both to preach. They were Brother Jimmy Miller and Brother Buford Miller. Both of them became great men of God. For years, Brother Jimmy pastored a Pentecostal Church in Hodge, Louisiana, and Brother Buford pastored the Pentecostal Church in Pascagoula, Mississippi. Both they and Brother Wily have gone on to be with the Lord.

I have already mentioned in this book my mother's brothers that God called to preach, Uncle Hiram, Uncle Matt, Uncle Wiley, as well as my daddy and my mother. I feel I have been compassed about with such a cloud of witnesses.

Uncle Matt fasted more days than he ate. I've known him to fast five days, eat one meal, and fast five more days. Many nights he would weep and pray all night. Once the Lord led him to California, and he caught the bus not knowing to just which church the Lord was sending him. Somewhere near Los Angeles, around one o'clock in the morning, the Holy Ghost revealed to him to ask the bus driver to let him off. Since there was no town or anything, the bus driver couldn't believe he wanted off. The bus pulled off, leaving him standing there on the side of the free-way. In a few minutes, a car stopped and the driver began inquiring who he was and where he was from. When Uncle Matt finished telling him, he said, "I pastor a church just a few miles away, and as I was in my office praying that God would send the evangelist to our church for a revival, the Spirit of the Lord spoke to me to get in my car, drive down the free-way, and I would find the preacher I needed."

During that revival fifty people received the Holy Ghost. This is just a sample of his ministry.

Chapter 4

My Wardrobe

My mother was a very good seamstress. Many times she made my dresses from clothing which had been given to her. I remember walking about a mile and a half to school with cardboard in my shoes to cover the holes in the soles. That same winter mother made me a coat out of cotton print and lined it with cotton outing. I would get so cold because the road would be iced over. Uncle Charlie Holland, Mother's brother, would laugh and say, "The difference between Mr. Sheff (a merchant in Bude) and me is that he has thin clothes and ice in the summer, and I have thin clothes and ice in the winter!"

The government began to help needy people. A family in the local community would be selected to store clothing in their home and to make the distributions. Daddy's sister and her husband were the "agency" in our community. One night that winter, one of my cousins invited me to spend the night. The next morning before we left for school, my aunt brought out a little gray cotton slipover sweater and gave it to me. I was thrilled beyond words. I was eight years old at the time. I'm sixty-seven now, but I have never forgotten that little gray sweater.

How I longed for high-heeled shoes to play in, but my mother never wore high heels. My cousin, Grace, and I came up with a unique improvisation. We would take empty thread spools, spread chewing gum all over one end, heat the gum with a lighted match, rub the spools together, and stick them on our bare heels! We would walk happily around for half a day before the spools began to become loose. Then we would reheat the gum! My mother would get upset because I had problems getting the gum off my heels.

Such great happiness came into my life one day when I went to town with Daddy. Bude was a very small town. We were in the store where Daddy and the owner talked as I stood by a table full of high-heeled shoes, looking longingly at them. Mr. Newman looked down at me and said, "Little Lady, would you like to have a pair of these shoes to play in?" I'm sure my face lit up as I exclaimed, "Yes, Sir!" He continued, "You can have as many pairs as you want." I began to think of my cousins who walked on spools, so I filled my arms with as many as I could carry. As I recall that joyous day, I am certain the shoes had gone out of style. I remember the toes were sharp. But it didn't matter at all; I had hit the jackpot for high heels. God sometimes drops handfuls on purpose for his own.

There are memories of embarrassment, too. On one occasion, I had gone home with a friend. Mother brought me a fresh dress to change into before church. Somehow we were late, so Mother urged, "Your dress is in the car. Just run out there and slip it on." It was already dark outside. I remember well the dress that Mother had brought, a pink taffeta hand-me-down from someone. It was a few sizes too big, and Mother had hurriedly made it fit by taking big seams in it. This type of unprofessional alteration was not her usual way, but the dress was lovely to me anyway. I hurried outside to our T-Model Ford where I slipped happily into my pretty dress. I entered the house feeling quite dressed up. I had been seated a few minutes before I looked down to notice that I had the dress on wrong side out, conspicuous wide seams and all!

I have many other memories of my wardrobe. I remember when there was only one church dress hanging in my wardrobe, and it had been given to me, a hand-me-down. Now, we are so blessed. Often, with a closet full of clothes, we are tempted to say, "I don't have anything to wear."

Chapter 5

Hard Times and Good Times – Mixed Together

Although children of my childhood days had few toys to play with, we always found something to do to have a good time. I remember how thrilled I would be when my parents would visit Uncle Wiley, my mother's brother, Aunt Eula and their family. Their oldest boy, G. W., was two or three years older than I and Jerry, the next son, was my age. Some younger brothers and sisters completed the happy group.

Uncle Wiley permitted G.W. to hook the mules to the wagon and take us for a ride. All the kids would pile into the wagon. G.W. always had to drive. As soon as we got out of sight of their house, he would make the mules run as fast as they could go. Sometimes we would be in the road and sometimes we would be just running across the hills with everybody just about to crack up laughing. Jerry, who was just like my very own brother, called G. W. "Bubber." When the wagon would get to going really fast, Jerry would be laughing so hard and screaming, "Bubber, Bubber." Surely an angel of the Lord was on the wagon with us, keeping someone from falling out and getting hurt.

Aunt Eula was a wonderful cook; the food at their house was delicious. Another thing that was so good was their cold milk, cooled by a spring about a block from their house. After milking the cows, Aunt Eula would pour the milk into big jars and carry them down the hill to place them in the cold water in the spring. In the evening for supper the cold milk would be such a special treat since people in the country didn't have ice boxes or refrigerators back then. So in the summer the milk was warm. If the cows had eaten bitter weeds, the milk would be bitter as well as warm.

Looking back now, I see the truth of the song, "Good Old Days." It was with us as it was when Jesus asked the disciples, "When I sent you without purse and script, did you lack anything?" They answered, "No, Lord, we didn't lack anything." It was because He sent His presence with them. Our home was filled with God's presence as we sang and praised and prayed. To the rich or poor, it's His presence that makes us happy.

Chapter 6

Laughter Turns to Silence

When I was a little girl one of the highlights of my life was visiting in the home of a great uncle and aunt, Uncle Will and Aunt Julia Wallace, who lived a few miles across the hills from my grandmother's. I loved going there with my grandmother and aunt. Travel was by either wagon or horse and buggy. One of the things that made the trip interesting was crossing a creek where there was no bridge. A few inches of crystal-clear water flowed over a bed of rocks. I can still see the water splashing around the feet of the horse, Old Frank, who was a gentle as a kitten. If he were thirsty, he would simply stop in the middle of the creek and enjoy a drink.

Aunt Julia and Uncle Will's house was on the other side of a steep hill. In the springtime everything was especially lovely with green grass, colorful flowers blooming, birds singing and bees working to fill their hives with honey. We would always find a covered dish filled with fresh honey in the comb on Aunt Julia's table.

In the fall of the year, I loved walking down the path to the syrup mill where the horses would be turning the mill and grinding the cane into juice. There would be much talk and laughter as Uncle Will and the boys cooked the syrup.

Years passed and I married and moved away. Very seldom did I have an opportunity to visit my aunts and uncles. After my grandmother passed away, Aunt Annie Bell continued living in the old home place. One day while I was visiting her, she mentioned that Uncle Will and Aunt Julia's children had decided to leave their parents' home just as it had been while they were living. This seemed strange to me.

After I went home, I would think about how I would love to go back out there one more time. Later when I was visiting my aunt, I asked if she thought the children would mind if we went to see the house. She assured me that they would not mind at all. This time we could not ride in the buggy; it was gone and Old Frank's bones were lying somewhere on the old place, bleached by the rain and sun. We were unable to cross the creek, but drove the car another way. We stopped by a son's house and picked up the key.

Things were so different; no birds were singing, no hens clucking and calling their little chicks to their sides, no roosters crowing, no bees working and filling the hives with honey, no dogs barking. Everything was quiet in the direction of the syrup mill. When we unlocked the front door, no one greeted us with a smiling face. Not a single footstep could be heard. The beds were covered with the old familiar spreads. Aunt Julia and Uncle Will's clothes were still hanging in the old wardrobe. His hat was hanging right where he hung it the last time he wore it and Aunt Julia's bonnet was in the place she had always kept it. Their shoes were in place. We looked around and then went to the dining room. There was the covered bowl for honey; it was empty. In the kitchen, it looked as if nothing had been moved since Aunt Julia had cooked their last meal. A box of soda and a can of baking powder remained there. There was also a half bottle of Watkins's vanilla flavoring that she always used in baking those delicious egg custards and big yellow cakes. Everything looked so lonely. I said to my aunt, "Let's go." It seemed this visit was erasing all the beautiful memories of yesterday.

These memories make me think of the terrible emptiness there will be in this world after the church is raptured. But those who are caught away into clouds of glory to that beautiful place called Heaven, where streets are pure gold and walls are of jasper, will forever be with the Lord. For those not ready for the Rapture, how will you feel in the tribulation following the rapture when the moon turns to blood, stars rain from the sky, and all water turns to blood? I warn you. Laughter will turn to silence. People will be crying and screaming throughout eternity.

Chapter 7

A Field of Love

When I was still in my teens, I felt the call of God so strong in my life. When I would stand to testify, such a heavy anointing would come upon me, I would just preach. My pastor told me, "I thought someday you would be my assistant here at the church."

I knew I had a call from God, but I felt so insufficient; I wondered how I could ever obey the Call. Little did I know that the Lord had someone he was going to put in my life that would encourage me to yield to this call.

A friend told me, "I had a dream about you, Agnes. I saw you walking across a beautiful green lawn and Brother Arlie Holmes was walking toward you singing a love song." A few days later, Brother Holmes, who

Sis. Holmes

My husband (A. O. Holmes) and I

was evangelizing at the time, arrived in the community where we lived. Somehow, it so happened that we were soon in each other's company. In the back of my mind, I kept thinking of that dream. Brother Holmes, tall, handsome, with special brown eyes, was kind-spoken and so dedicated to the Lord. It was no wonder that I enjoyed his company more than I had ever enjoyed the company of any other young man. I was nineteen years old and had dated some nice young men, but never before had I felt as happy as I did with this special person.

Brother Holmes hardly missed a revival. He and his two little girls, Juanita and Arlene, had been evangelizing since the angels of the Lord had come and taken their mother to Heaven. Both girls had long hair, and Brother Holmes would get some of the saints to braid it for them.

We saw each other a few times, and then it was time for him to leave. We had a little talk before he left, with Brother Holmes doing most of the talking. I was aware that he had been dating another young lady, but I wasn't sure of his feeling for her. I'll never forget the words he said, "If you see someone else you want to go with, you feel free to, and I'll do the same. Is that all right with you?"

I was shocked but managed to reply, "All right." And that's the way we parted. I thought, "He surely doesn't feel about me the way I feel about him," but I was able to put on a good front. While he was away, I dated someone else, making sure that his sister knew about it. When he returned from his revival, I didn't know what to expect. But one thing was for sure, I knew that he had heard how things had gone while he was away.

About the first time we were together again he said, "I feel different than I did when I talked to you before I left. Let me make a suggestion. If you won't date anyone else, I won't!" I was thrilled with this suggestion. I imagine I felt as Ruth did when she heard Boaz say, "Go not to another field. Abide fast by my servants."

My husband (A.O. Holmes) and I

We stood before Mr. Loyd Dillon, Justice of the Peace, to say our marriage vows. Brother Holmes's sister, Lexie, was with us. Since my parents felt that I was too young to take on the responsibility of a husband with two little girls, six-year-old Arlene and nine-year-old Juanita, we just slipped quietly away. Mother and Daddy cried and didn't sleep all night.

24

We found ourselves in that field of love where we would labor together for more than forty years, enjoying the presence of God and the company of each other. We were so happy with each other. Those dear little girls were never anything but a blessing. My parents became convinced that Brother Holmes was one of the greatest sons-in-law who ever lived. (He really was!)

After we were married, we went to Uncle Wiley Holland's house. He said, "Agnes, I think it's wonderful you two are married, and let me tell you this: if you never do anything but be a mother to these two little girls, you will be doing a great work for God." Well, I'm sure I wasn't a perfect step-mother, and I'm sure I made a lot of mistakes, but we were happy, and there was love. We were poor, but we were always happy and enjoyed life. When we married, they all three made me welcome, opening their home and hearts to me.

For the first years after Brother Holmes and I were married, we evangelized. The Lord blessed, giving us souls during revivals. Times were very hard. There wasn't very much money, but I don't believe I could have been any happier if I had owned a million dollars. I had the joy of salvation and I loved Brother Holmes. As a matter of fact, everyone that knew Brother Holmes loved him.

We went through some trials and walked through some dark valleys, but there was always love and respect for each other. It seems I can still hear him say, "Come on; leave what you're doing and just ride with me." It would be to the store or, often, to the hospital to visit someone. Even on a dark, stormy day, if we could just be together, it seemed the sun was shining.

I remember when I was young and began to think that some day when I married, I wanted to marry someone older so I wouldn't have to feel very much responsibility. That's exactly what the Lord had for me. Brother Holmes was so dear and had such love and was so caring. I remember one time Juanita made the remark, "There isn't anyone like Daddy." He didn't only love us but he loved everyone and always had such compassion.

The offerings received in revivals were little more than enough to get us to the next one, and many

My husband (A. O. Holmes), and I
Juanita and Arlene

25

Ruebel and I

times food was not very plentiful. But the glory and the blessings of the Lord made up for it all because in His presence is fullness of joy. I remember once while in revival we didn't have any meat to cook. I got so hungry for some kind of meat. We hadn't been married long and I was a little bashful. Finally, I got enough nerve to ask Bro. Holmes if we could afford to buy a can of salmon that would cost less than twenty-five cents. He just looked at me never saying a word. I was so embarrassed; that I wished I had never mentioned desiring meat.

We evangelized for a year or so and ended up in Jayess, Mississippi. Brother Holmes was elected pastor, and we settled down. It was while we were living in the little parsonage there, after we had been married two-and-half years, that God blessed us with a sweet little boy. His daddy named him Ruebel Vaiden.

Arlene and Juanita were so thrilled he was a boy because their little brother had gone home to be with the Lord when he was two years and eight months old. Juanita would say, "I'll feel better when Ruebel gets past that age."

After living in Jayess for two-and-a-half years, we moved to Biloxi, Mississippi, where we built a church. We had great revivals there for a year-and-a-half. They sang that old song, "Everybody Will Be Happy Over There," but we were happy down here. We met many new friends and saw great revivals. One of our highlights was camp meeting, especially in Urania, Louisiana, where Brother Hooter was the chief cook. We enjoyed the good food but especially the wonderful services.

Within the next few days, the Lord provided meat. We had our little home on wheels parked by the church having services every night. A family invited us to go home with them to spend the night. They didn't have a car and lived a mile or two from the church. We all walked with them to their home after church and spent the night. When nearing the house truck after walking home the next day, we noticed a package lying on the steps. It was a big round steak.

I gained a lot of experience cooking and doing the laundry for my new little family, and I enjoyed every minute of it. In one experience I had with the laundry, I learned a lesson I never forgot. As the saying is, experience is the best teacher. Since I wanted Brother Holmes, Juanita and Arlene to look their best, I made cold water starch, which was very stiff starch. The only problem was, clothes had to be dipped in the starch and ironed while completely wet. I ironed the clothes for hours since they had to be ironed until they were dry. I remember Brother Holmes asking, "What are you doing?" I imagine sometimes with some of my foolish ways, he must have thought, "Now I don't only have two children to raise, but three."

My husband, Ruebel, and I

Ruebel and I

27

Chapter 8

Hearing His Voice – Obeying His Leading

From early childhood, my mother made such a deep impression upon me concerning the fear of the Lord and obedience to His leading. She taught me to hear His voice and to do what He told me to do.

Sister Evelyn Reed, a precious saint in the New Bethel Church (Jayess, Mississippi), where Brother Holmes pastored, gave this testimony. During the Depression when jobs could hardly be found, she, then a young woman, had moved from far north to this community where she met and married Mr. Dewey Reed. Not long afterward, her neighbor invited her to go with her to the revival that was in progress at the Pentecostal church.

This was the first time she had ever heard of Pentecost. She was so greatly impressed the first night that she went back the next night. When the altar call was given, she went to the altar. She had never seen anyone pray in the altar or receive the Holy Ghost; but as she dropped to her knees, she began to feel the presence of the Lord. In her mind she could see a picture of the Lord carrying a lamb in his arms and a number of sheep following Him. She began saying, "Lord, take me! Lord, take me!" The Holy Ghost fell on her and she began speaking in tongues.

Not long after this revival ended, the pastor had another evangelist and his family to come and preach a revival. Since they had a trailer, the pastor announced a pounding for them. Sister Reed said that when she began to pray the next morning, she thought that she'd like to take the preacher five pounds of sugar, but then she remembered she didn't even have a grain of sugar herself and no money to buy any.

During those days there was a grocery truck that came through each week. It would be an old school bus with shelves and perhaps chicken coops built on the outside. Customers could trade chickens and eggs for groceries. As it happened that day was the day for it to come by, but she remembered her hens had stopped laying.

She prayed, "Lord, help me to have something to take to the evangelist tonight." All at once the Holy Ghost impressed her to go and gather some new straw and put it in the hens' nests. She got up from praying, rushed out back, and began pulling straw for the nest. After the second handful, she saw a nest full of eggs! The hens had stolen their nest out and had been laying, but she didn't know about it. She ran into the kitchen, got a pan, picked up the eggs, and counted them. It was just enough to buy the evangelist five pounds of sugar.

She was so excited and happy, she decided she would go ahead and put new straw in the nests anyway. By the time the grocery bus came in the afternoon, the hens had laid enough eggs in their nests of new straw to buy five pounds of sugar for herself, also.

God is the same God that sent Elijah down to the widow woman's house. She was gathering sticks to cook the last meal for her and her son to eat before their death. The prophet of the Lord said, "Cook me one first." She obeyed and as long as the famine lasted, the cruse of oil and the barrel of meal never failed.

One night while we were in services at Bethel, Brother Dunaway came late when the service was almost over, but Brother Holmes wanted him to say something. As Brother Holmes talked to him, Brother Dunaway failed to realize that Brother Holmes was turning his necktie all the way to the back. Brother Dunaway rose to speak and right away felt the anointing, oblivious to the flying necktie beating his back. He couldn't understand why people were laughing. He didn't find out until after he had sat down. "Brother Holmes!" he exclaimed.

Uncle Hiram and Aunt Sally lived in Vicksburg, Mississippi, where he pastored a church. Every few months Brother Holmes would let me visit his church for a few nights of revival. All three of my preacher uncles were so kind to both Brother Holmes and me; they treated me more like a daughter than a niece.

One time while I was in revival at Vicksburg, we kept fasting and praying but we just couldn't seem to get a spiritual breakthrough. I'll never forget one morning when Aunt Sally and I were in the house and every now and then the power of God would get in my hands. I would clap them really fast; in a few minutes I'd do the same thing again. I said, "Aunt Sally, we must be going to get a breakthrough tonight. I feel something special in my hands!"

Sure enough, that's exactly what the Holy Ghost was telling us.

That night Heaven kissed that little Pentecostal church on the side of the hill. Six grown people received the Holy Ghost! One of them was Uncle Hiram's son-in-law, Brother Dennis Lambert. Well, it was a "little Pentecost," which was "noised abroad." We worshipped so loud a neighbor called the police. The police came out and attempted to quiet us down, but we had all gotten drunk in the Spirit and just continued to worship.

The next morning a woman swore out a warrant against Uncle Hiram. The police came, arrested him, and locked him up in jail. If you don't think that looked unusual, a preacher in a suit, white shirt, and tie standing in a cell! Someone paid his bond and he was out in time for the next service.

Later, he was brought to trial. When the woman who had him arrested testified on the witness stand, she said, "Well, Judge, it wasn't really the noise that bothered me so, but the kind of noise."

I was praying and seeking the Lord when He spoke to me to go to Sister Edna Wallace's home. She lived about eight or ten miles away. She was a minister and she attended the church at Pine Grove. I did not know why the Holy Ghost was sending me, but I felt I must hurry to her house. Since my mother lived between Sister Wallace's house and my house, I carried my baby to mother's and told her to keep him while I went to see what the Lord was sending me for. When I got there, Sister Wallace said, "My baby is bad sick and looks like he's going to die. I prayed about an hour or two ago asking God if he had anyone He could talk to and send to my home to pray for the child."

Well, the Lord healed her little boy. I'm so glad God hears our cry. I was so glad that day that I heard His voice and obeyed. God works on both ends of the line. Thank God for His healing power.

I felt such a burden to pray this one particular day while Bro. Holmes was helping the brothers work on the well there in Bethel. The Spirit of the Lord brought a pastor's wife before me and said, "I want you to go and tell her that I want her to become more humble." I felt such an urgency to go right away that when Brother Holmes stepped into the parsonage a few minutes later, I asked him if he could make the fifty or sixty mile trip right then.

"I can't go now. I want to help these brothers, but I'll take you in the morning."

A few miles before we arrived the following morning, I said to Bro. Holmes, "This message the Lord has given me is not going to be easy to say."

"You'd better obey God," replied Bro. Holmes. I began praying for God to help me, and He really did. He went before me. The pastor's wife met us on the front porch and said, "Your coming is not a surprise. I dreamed last night that you were coming and on the way you said to Bro. Holmes, 'This message the Lord has given me is not going to be easy to say,' and Bro. Holmes said, 'You had better obey God.'"

The Lord fixed it; He made it easy for me to obey the Lord when He spoke the words to her in a dream before I ever spoke them. She said, "Come on in. We have a very sick baby." (We had not heard that the little two-year-old girl had been sick.) We found her lying in bed, her little body swollen all over. They told us, "She has not been able to eat solid foods for three weeks-liquids only." I told the pastor and his wife the words that the Lord had given me.

We prayed, believing the Lord would raise her up. We spent the night with them. The next morning there was no change. The baby was still very ill, and she was burning with fever. We dreaded to leave, but Bro. Holmes was also pastoring Pine Grove Church and there was a fellowship meeting that night.

We drove to the home of one of the saints near the church. There was a grove of trees near the house. I told Bro. Holmes, "I'm going to pray out there." It was a custom that each preacher would have about five minutes to speak, and I was thinking about the service. As I was praying, the Lord revealed to me, "They are coming-bringing the sick baby!" It shocked me.

I started back to the house, and just as I was entering through the gate, they drove up. One of their saints was sitting in the back seat with

Pine Grove Pentecostal Church in the 1930's

31

the little girl, who was lying on some pillows. When the sister stepped out of the car, she whispered to me "Sis. Holmes, I thought every mile of the way she would die." She was still burning with fever.

It was near sundown when all went into the church for service. After the service had begun, all at once quietness came over the church and the presence of the Lord came down really strong. Sister Oath Price, a very spiritual member of the church, fasted and prayed much. When she entered the church, I don't believe she ever got more than two feet from the front door before the power of God would come upon her. She always came down the aisle speaking in tongues. In the quietness of this service, she suddenly stood speaking in tongues and walking across the aisle to the sick baby, who was lying on pillows at her mother's side. I can still remember the words she was saying in another tongue-some of the same words she would speak when she entered the church door each service. She laid hands on that dying little girl, and sweat began to dampen her little face. She was healed!

Sister Sartin invited them to her home to spend the night. For breakfast the next morning, she made homemade biscuits. The little girl went to the table and ate biscuits and syrup-her first solid food in three weeks. She went home after breakfast—healed! This was one of the greatest miracles I have ever witnessed.

During the time Brother Holmes pastored the church at Bethel, near Jayess, Mississippi, we were so happy. The saints were so kind to us that we hoped we would never have to leave. One morning as I was praying

Bethel Church at Jayess, Mississippi

in the little parsonage, the Spirit of the Lord revealed to me a little trailer owned by my brother who lived about seventy-five miles away. The Lord said, "I want you to buy it." When Brother Holmes came in, I began very excitedly to tell him what the Lord had said, but I quickly realized that he did not share my excitement. He said that we had neither use for a trailer, nor money to buy it. My excitement undampened, I persuaded him to let me write a penny postcard to my brother to find out if the trailer was for sale and if so, what he would take for it. Touched by my burden, Brother Holmes agreed.

The answer came in a few days: the trailer was for sale and the price was twenty-five dollars. The problem was that we did not have the twenty-five dollars. I felt, however, that God had said to buy it and that we must do whatever He said.

We were in a fellowship-meeting circle of neighboring churches that met once a month. The next meeting was at our church. It was a custom that an offering be given to the host pastor. That night the Lord blessed in a special way: the offering was thirty dollars! I told Brother Holmes, "There is the twenty-five dollars for the trailer and five dollars for gas." I persuaded him to buy the trailer.

Brother Holmes parked the little sixteen-foot homemade trailer in front of our house. When people asked about it, Brother Holmes would say, "That's my wife's trailer." One Sunday Brother and Sister Cecil Reed, who attended a neighboring church, came to visit. Brother Reed asked about the trailer and offered to buy it for fifty dollars. "Why don't you sell it?" asked Brother Holmes. "No, I had better not sell it," I told him, becoming embarrassed from all of the teasing. After that, he never teased me about the trailer again.

A few weeks later, Brother Holmes was in the church praying while I was in the parsonage with our two little girls and our little nine-month-old boy. Brother Holmes walked into the house and said, "The Lord has just spoken to me to resign this church and to go to Biloxi, Mississippi." Brother Holmes had received invitations to pastor other churches if he ever felt his work was finished at Bethel. We did not know a living soul in Biloxi and had never been invited there.

Brother Holmes resigned the church the following Saturday night. We put our few clothes in the little trailer and left the next morning. It was September, 1944; the weather was hot and there was no air-conditioning; however, we were used to the heat since we had never had air-conditioning in the church or the parsonage.

The tires on the trailer were worn and we had many flats. I can't remember how many times that Juanita, Arlene, Reubel and I would find shade under a tree and wait while Brother Holmes fixed a flat.

We arrived in Biloxi late Sunday evening. Brother Holmes just drove in the direction he felt, like Abraham, not knowing where he was going. He drove down Division Street, turning the corner on Crawford Street and stopped in front of a small house where a family was sitting on the front porch. The man walked out to the car, and Brother Holmes asked him if he knew any Pentecostals. "Yes, we are," he replied.

Our new friend, Brother Woods, told his wife to bring us a pitcher of ice water. That was the first thing cold which we had had to drink that day. Forty dollars was all the money we had so we felt that we could not buy soft drinks, although the price for one was only a dime. (All the members of the church we had left were farmers who could not pay tithes until the cotton was harvested and sold. We left at the beginning of harvest, before tithes were paid. The Lord knew what He was doing. My uncle, Hiram Holland, accepted the church and he would need the tithes for the winter.) Many years have passed, but I have never forgotten how refreshing that pitcher of ice water was, how it satisfied our thirst.

Brother and Sister Woods invited us to attend a tent revival with them that night over on Back Bay. Brother Charlie Herring, the evangelist, invited Brother Holmes to preach a few nights under the tent but Brother Holmes faced a difficulty. Brother Herring felt it better not to be too noisy and not to give an altar call. Brother Holmes preached God-sent conviction and invited those who felt the Lord was calling them to come and shake his hand. Sinners began coming. The next night, Brother Holmes could take it no longer. He gave an altar call and the altar filled. It seems we never did get a real breakthrough, however, and the tent was taken down soon after that.

Brother Holmes was invited by a Brother Hankins to attend a small church on Crawford Street so we moved our little trailer by the church. There was no pastor but Brother Loften from Jonesville, Louisiana, was there preaching a revival. Our little trailer leaked, and it rained every night. Brother Holmes would stop to repair the leaks between showers, but he evidently didn't have the right materials because the leaking continued. When the sun came out, we hung the wet clothes on a fence to dry.

Not many were coming to the services, but all was not disappointment. A delightful change for us was cereal for breakfast. Another treat we loved was bologna sandwiches. We did not have a stove, but we had an electric icebox. Now we could buy milk and keep it cold. Back in Bethel we had a small icebox in which ice was placed, but nothing stayed very cold. Another difference was that in Bethel I had to milk the cow. Although the cow was gentle, there were problems. One of her teats had a hole in its side that caused warm milk to spray on me as I milked. Also, she had cockleburs in the end of her tail, which she switched when bitten by horseflies, and scratched me.

When Brother Loften closed the revival and returned home, the man in charge asked Brother Holmes to preach a few nights. Just a few people came for services. I have to admit we became discouraged. Brother Holmes thought things over and came up with an idea. "Let's go to the Mississippi Delta, pick cotton, get some clothes, and evangelize," he said. "That's all I know to do." "Picking cotton" seemed almost like a bad word to me.

Some people from Saucier, about twenty miles from Biloxi, came to the revival and invited Brother Holmes to preach there. Brother Holmes said, "We will stop at Saucier Saturday and Sunday nights, and we'll leave Monday for the Delta."

The biggest rain of all came Saturday night before time for service. We were in the church praying for the service and found that the church leaked worse than our trailer. Only one place in the church was dry— down the aisle. Every one of the unpadded, homemade pews were soaked. Not one single person came to church; they knew the church would be wet and were used to being rained out. I said, "Looks like God is trying to drown us."

I felt so depressed, facing a long trip the next morning — and not a sightseeing trip, either. It would consist of wading through the dew, getting wet to our necks in the morning, scorching sun by noon, cotton burrs pricking our fingers until they bled, a narrow strap cutting into our shoulders from pulling forty or more pounds of cotton, and some bologna sandwiches to eat as the sun beat down on our backs.

When we went into the trailer, Brother Holmes didn't seem too disturbed. He lay down across the bed and began to play with the baby. I asked Juanita and Arlene if they wanted to pray. As we knelt there on the floor, the Holy Ghost took over and showed me a vision. I saw a well flowing with clear water and people coming to drink. The Holy Ghost spoke, "Go back to Biloxi. People are hungry, and they will come."

We went back to that same little church which we had left. Within a week, God sent a revival that lasted for seven months. God blessed us every way we turned and we built a much larger church.

People brought us oysters by the gallon, shrimp, ham and chicken and we were blessed with new clothes. The Lord gave us a house on Howard Street with five acres of land. It was during World War II, and wives of soldiers were looking for places to live. We rented the trailer and Brother Holmes gave me the rent.

A short time after we moved to Biloxi, I was in prayer one day when the Spirit of the Lord revealed to me to go to a little country church about ninety miles away. Since I knew the pastor Brother Dexter Rushing, I wrote a penny postcard telling him that the Holy Ghost had moved on me to go to his church. Several days passed, but no answer came. Feeling so insufficient anyway, I felt that I would not have to go since he did not answer my card.

A few days passed, and the Holy Ghost moved on me again to go. I said, "Lord, I wish I had just gone and not written. I will feel so embarrassed to drive up to their gate." The Spirit of the Lord showed me to go to Bethel and He would send Brother Rushing there.

When I told Brother Holmes, he said, "They are having a fellowship meeting Friday night at Bethel. I'll take you." During the meeting, I kept looking for Brother and Sister Rushing. I asked Sister Janice if Brother and Sister Rushing came very often. She answered, "No. Since they began pastoring, they don't come very often." I thought, Lord, I don't understand.

In just a few minutes Sister Janice came back and said, "Sister Holmes, I didn't know it, but some of the family said that Brother Rushing had called during the service." One of their relatives had died in Tyler Town Hospital, and they were on their way there.

The next morning we drove over to the home of Brother Rushing's mother-in-law. As Brother Rushing approached us in our car, I said, "Brother Holmes, you ask him." I felt so relieved when he said, "I will." Brother Holmes told him, "My wife feels a burden to go and be in service at your church."

"I got your card," he said, " and I hate I neglected to answer it."

Brother Holmes, Juanita, Arlene, and Reubel went back to Biloxi for the weekend service there. I told Brother Holmes I'd catch the bus and be home Monday.

Brother Rushing had young people's service that Saturday night. There was no Sunday school the following morning, but there was a special service that afternoon in another church. When they invited me to go, I told them I believed I'd just stay there.

After they left, I went to a pasture behind the house and began praying. I felt such a burden on that hot fall day in October. I began crying, begging the Lord, "If you are not going to fill at least one, I want you to let me die here on this grass."

It seemed the Lord answered, "Would you be willing to die and leave your baby?" (He was about ten or eleven months old.)

I said, "Yes, I'm willing." And they will never know why you died I thought, but I assured the Lord that if He was not going to fill at least one soul, I wanted to die. I went back to the parsonage.

When service began that night, there was a new face — a young mother from that community who belonged to the Baptist church. She had never before been in a Pentecostal church. When the altar call was given, she came to the altar, where she received the baptism of the Holy Ghost speaking in other tongues just as they did on the day of Pentecost. The church came alive! And I was rejoicing with them!

"Sister Holmes," the pastor exclaimed, "this is the first one to receive the Holy Ghost this year." And it was October. He continued, "If I hadn't already planned to go to the conference, we would start a revival."

I felt the peace of God as I left happily the next morning to catch the bus to Biloxi.

Thirty years passed and I was at Brother and Sister Cox's church in Pine, Louisiana, when a young man came to me after church and said, "My grandmother told me to ask you if you are the Sister Holmes that was preaching at Brother Rushing's church when she got the Holy Ghost." I replied, "I am the same Sister Holmes."

She had lived to see her children and grandchildren receive the Holy Ghost!

Chapter 9

God Sends Another Trailer

The Lord woke me up one morning before daybreak to get up and pray. While I was in the Spirit, the Lord reminded me of a trailer that I had heard was for sale. He impressed me that He wanted me to go and look at it. I didn't have money to buy a trailer, and as far as I knew, we had no use for one. But as Mother always said, "If the Lord tells you something to do, you have got to obey Him." It still wasn't daylight, but I woke up Brother Holmes to tell him that I had to go look at this trailer. Brother Holmes just said, "Come back and lie down."

That morning I kept asking him, "Will you take me?"

"I don't have any money to buy a trailer, and I don't think I need one," he answered.

"I know we can't buy it, but I have to go look at it," I replied.

Finally, he said, "I'll take you, but you have to promise me you won't ask me to buy it in front of the owners and embarrass me." I said, "I promise. All I'll do is look at it. I won't say one word."

When we arrived at the owner's house, she was busy preparing supper. She gave Brother Holmes the key so that we could go alone to look at the trailer. When we stepped inside, I saw that it was beautiful, but true to my promise, I said nothing and prepared to leave.

While we were in the trailer, the woman's husband came home from work. Brother Holmes went to return the key, and the couple followed him to the car. "Brother Holmes," he said, "I have been working in the shipyard making good money, but I haven't paid any tithes. We owe the Lord more than this, but we want to give this trailer to you and Sister Holmes." Neither one of them had the Holy Ghost.

We never did live in the trailer but parked it in the yard beside our other little trailer and rented it to a soldier's wife. When the Lord led us to North Little Rock, Arkansas, we sold the trailer. With the money from its sale, plus some of our savings, we were able to pay cash for a new 1947 Chevrolet. We had never before been able to afford a new car. The Lord truly "works in mysterious ways His wonders to perform." Whatever He tells us to do, we must obey Him. I'm so glad my mother drilled that into me as a child.

My husband and Ruebel

My parents Byrd and Ida Clark, Ruebel, and I

My husband, Juanita, Arlene, Ruebel, and I

Chapter 10

✝

Second and Buckeye

When we first came to North Little Rock, the church didn't have a pastor. There was just a very small congregation, maybe twenty-five, counting all the children. We had left Biloxi in the middle of a great revival that had lasted for about seven months. The Lord sent this good revival, then said, "Move on somewhere else."

I thought of the scripture that says, " . . . look on the fields; for they are white already to harvest" (John 4:35). As we look through our eyes, we just can't see that the fields are white. They just don't look white to us as they look white to God.

There was a lady in the church, Sister Martin, who had the Holy Ghost but none of her family did. Her oldest son, Carroll, who lived out in the country, had married a girl from the Baptist church. Before they got married, her parents said, "Violet, if you marry him, he will drag you into that Pentecostal stuff." She told Brother Carroll what her parents had said, and he told her, "I promise you, Violet, that I will never ask you to go to a Pentecostal church."

After they were married, they liked to go dancing every Saturday night. They had a beautiful little girl and when she was about four years old Sister Violet would dress her up in beautiful clothes and place her upon a table while she and Brother Carroll danced. Just a few months before we came to North Little Rock, the Lord called this little girl to Heaven, and it took all the joy out of their dancing. They did not want to go back to the Saturday night dances.

About this time there was a revival at the Baptist church in the community, and Brother Carroll said, "Let's go!" He had made up his mind that he was going to join the Baptist Church. They went to church that Sunday morning, and he and Sister Violet both walked up to the front with the others, and Brother Carroll joined the church. The preacher told them to repeat what he said. They repeated the preacher's words, and when they were finished, right in front of the whole congregation, Brother Carroll said, "Is this all I get?" (He was very outspoken.)

The preacher asked, "What do you mean?"

Brother Carroll replied, "Well, I don't feel a bit different."

The preacher moved a little closer to Brother Carroll and said, "I want to talk to you behind the church after the service is over." (In those days not many churches had an office. "Behind the church" was the office!) Brother Carroll followed him outside and the preacher said, "You're not going to get what you're looking for in this church. You'll have to go to one of those 'holiness' churches."

One day a few weeks after this happened, his mother said to him, "Carroll, we're having a revival at Second and Buckeye. There's a preacher there with a drum, and people are receiving the Holy Ghost. I want you to go."

He told Sister Violet, "My word is just as good as it was the day I first told you I would never ask you to go to a Pentecostal church, but I'm going tonight."

She replied, "Well, if you go, I'm going, too."

They came that night, and on the way home he said, "Violet, I'm going back tomorrow night. If I feel what I felt tonight, I'm going to the altar."

She answered, "I'm going back, too."

The next night, it happened! When Brother Carroll started walking to the altar, Sister Violet was right behind him. They actually received the Holy Ghost **at the same time**! It was such a wonderful night for us. That was part of the "field" that God could see that we couldn't see. When they quit rejoicing, they met each other and started speaking in tongues again. This was part of the beginning of the church on Buckeye Street.

Sometime after Brother Carroll and Sister Violet Martin received the Holy Ghost, the Lord spoke to me to go to their home. Brother Carroll had been feeling a call to the ministry and I felt that God had a message for him.

Brother Holmes drove me to their home in the country about twenty miles away. When we arrived about two o'clock that afternoon and asked Sister Violet where Brother Carroll was, she replied, "He is plowing on a tractor about five miles away and won't be home until late this evening. I can go with you and show you where he is."

A feeling came over me, however, to just wait a little while. A few minutes later Brother Carroll drove up, saying, "The tractor broke down."

I told him, "The Lord has spoken for us to come, but I don't know why. Let's pray."

41

As we bowed on our knees, the Lord began to speak, "I have called thee to come out from thy kindred." Again the Spirit spoke saying, "Nine, nine, I see nine."

Brother Martin and Brother Blasingame, who pastored a church in Conway, had jointly rented a farm, borrowing money to plant the crop. Brother Martin said, "If the Lord will allow me to get this crop in, I'll never farm again."

The Lord blessed the crop. After it was harvested, Brother Martin bought a travel trailer and prepared to drive to Mississippi for his first revival. He pulled the trailer and parked it by our house to spend the night before they left. Although none of us had thought of it before, in the morning we remembered the number nine which the Holy Ghost had spoken during the prayer meeting at the Martins' farm. It was nine months to the day that the tractor had broken down and the Lord had sent him from the fields to meet us.

There was a woman who lived in town, Sister Pauline Shelby, who had been coming to the revival but had never made a move towards the altar. I didn't really know her; I just knew her face. I was washing dishes late one evening and I began to feel the Spirit of the Lord. (All you Pentecostal mothers know that whenever you're in the Spirit, you wash and iron easier.) The Lord put this woman's face before me. The Holy Ghost gave me an urgent feeling, "Go now! Go to her home!" I found Brother Holmes and I said, "The Lord has spoken to me to go to this woman's home."

He said, "You're going to make us late for church."

"I've got to go," I replied, "You can just drive around the block once and I'll be ready to leave." I talked him into it.

When we arrived at her house, she was standing outside washing clothes on a rub board. It was late in the evening and she still had a lot of washing to do, lying there on the ground. I didn't know what to tell her because I didn't know why I had come. I saw all that laundry and thought, "God, did you send me here to help her wash?"

She said, "I'll put all this down and we'll go into the house."

I said, "No, I'll just help you wash."

"Oh, no," she replied, "You go on into the house." She wanted me to go into the house first, and I didn't know why. I later learned that she had snuff in her mouth and wanted to get it out of her mouth. I had been under the impression that only elderly people used snuff, but she was just a young woman. She insisted that I go on ahead of her.

I thought, "God, I don't know what to tell her. I don't know why I'm here." She stepped into the house right behind me. I looked at her and she looked at me. Finally, I said, "I was praying, and the Lord revealed to

42

me to come to your house. Let's pray!" I didn't know if she would pray or not, but I just fell on my knees and started praying. I've always felt that when you don't know what to do, pray. I knew it wouldn't take Brother Holmes very long to drive around the block; he would be out front soon, sounding the horn for me. I started praying and she got down on her knees. I decided to check to see what she was doing, and when I looked around, I saw tears running down her cheeks. I started praying with her, and in just a few minutes she was filled with the Holy Ghost. I got it over again, too! About that time, I heard a horn sounding out front. I was so happy when I stepped out on that front porch. I told Brother Holmes, "Come on in; she's got the Holy Ghost!"

After we moved to Little Rock, the Lord led me to preach a few nights in Biloxi. I took my daughter Sharon, who was then three or four years old, and we picked up my mother on the way. We spent the nights in an evangelist's bedroom near the Sunday school rooms in the church.

On Sunday evening, I called Brother Holmes to tell him I would be closing that night and would be home the next day. After church when we were in our bedroom, a feeling came over me to call home. When I mentioned this to my mother, she offered to go with me to the phone in the church. At the time I did not know why I had the urge to call since I had already called just a few hours earlier. But I was to learn in a short time.

After we had returned to bed, I heard the sound of footsteps coming down the hall. I had always been a "scaredy cat", but I had never seen my mother afraid until that night. She said, "That's Brother Springer coming to get ice in the church kitchen." I knew Brother Springer would not want to frighten us, so I called his name several times, but there was no answer.

"Mother, it's not Brother Springer," I said. I got up and went to the one door in our room; feeling led to pray over it. Just after we prayed, I heard someone breathing really hard just outside the door. The door fastener was one that could have easily been unlocked. It came to me to lay my hand on the facings of the door in Jesus' name. Mother went to the one window and began calling Brother Springer. I was so frightened I said, "Mother, come put your hand on the door facing, and I'll see if I can get the

Sharon, Mother and I

43

window raised and make them hear me." I held my hand securely until she placed hers there. Sharon, who had been standing by me, moved to stand by mother.

Although Mother was quite hard-of-hearing, she said, "I hear him breathing." By this time, I felt that I could faint, but I got that window up and turned up the volume. I scared Mother worse than the prowler did. She told me later that she had been afraid that I would have a heart attack. As I called, lights began coming on across the street.

I continued to call, "Brother Springer!" Then I'd scream, "Call the police." Mother said, "They're not going to hear you!" But I just screamed louder.

Because the wind was blowing, Brother and Sister Springer could not distinguish our voices. They thought that they were hearing the sound of people just carrying on. And then at last Brother Springer realized that they were hearing our voices. "Jump up, Betty. That's Sister Clark. Sister Holmes must have fallen."

At the same time the thought came to my mind to just pretend Brother Springer had heard. I calmed down and cried, "Yes, call the police," whereupon the man ran from our door, slamming the outside door as he went out. With great relief, Mother said, "He's gone!"

Minutes later the police arrived. A neighbor had heard me and had called them. The policeman said, "They were after money."

"Do you get many calls like this?" I asked. "Just from eight to ten a night," he answered.

My usually brave mother said that when she walked out of the room, her knees were knocking together. I told Brother Springer that I would never again stay in the evangelist's quarters. We went into the Springers' home to spend the remainder of the night.

Brother Springer told us that an extra doorstop had been put on the door which we entered to use the phone, and I had failed to really close the door after using the phone. If the intruder had been unable to enter through that door, he would have come through a window down by the kitchen, and we would have never heard him! The Lord was watching over us.

I don't remember how long it was before we went back to Biloxi for a revival, but Brother and Sister Springer told us when we got there, "We're going to stay at the church, and you all can have our house."

A big revival broke out and many received the Holy Ghost. Revival services continued every night for five weeks. When it was over, Sister Springer said, "I won't ever again move out of my house and stay at the church." I laughed. I could not blame her.

When I got home from Biloxi, Brother Joel was in Silsbee, Texas, preaching a revival for Brother Duplissey. He had called for his daddy and me to come and be with him. Brother Holmes said, "I can't go, Mama. You go and be with him a couple of nights." Brother Jackie Beard, in our church, who was sixteen years old at the time, went with me.

Can you believe that I had an experience there similar to the one I endured in Biloxi! Brother Duplissey had bedrooms for evangelists at the church and he lived across the street. Brother Jackie and Brother Joel were in the room next to mine. Not long after I got to my room, I heard a noise by my window. I called to Brother Joel, and he called to Brother Duplissey. He and Brother Hair came from across the street to our rescue. They found that the screen on my window had been removed! You can believe that I spent the night with Brother and Sister Duplissey.

When I told Brother Holmes about the experience, he said, "That's the Devil just trying to scare you." "He's making a pretty good job at it," I said.

Brother Holmes, who was never afraid of anything, had never owned a gun of any kind. The first gun to ever be in our home was after Brother Joe Duke had preached a revival. He preached about the Mark of the Beast and said that saints would be hiding in the woods and would have to kill animals to eat. Brother Joel, who was then fourteen, said to me one day after the revival had closed, "Mother, come here. I want to show you something." He was standing in his room holding a gun. "You remember," he said, "how Brother Duke was preaching about the Mark of the Beast. I went and bought this gun."

Chapter 11

Revival Memories

The Lord blessed in a great way and the church began to grow. Even though Brother Holmes was now pastoring a big church in North Little Rock, the Spirit often moved on me to go somewhere for a few nights' revival. Brother Holmes was always so understanding and helped me to obey the Lord in every way he could.

One time the Lord led me to Sheridan, Arkansas, which was only forty miles from North Little Rock, so I drove back and forth every night. We were also having a revival at home in which five men were preaching (Brother Mayo, three of his sons and another brother). I cooked for them, laundered their clothes, and was just as happy as I could be. One night Brother Joel, who was six months old, cried the whole forty miles to

Sis. Holmes

Sheridan, but the Lord blessed and sixteen people received the Holy Ghost. Brother Holmes came to Sheridan one service and baptized them.

When Ruebel, my older son, was about four years old, I felt led of the Lord to go to Brother Jones's church in Jigger, Louisiana, for a few nights. I took Reubel with me and we rode the bus there.

The first night we were there Aunt Adelia, my mother's sister who was in that church, approached me and said, "I want you to stay with me while you are here." I was thrilled since I had not even seen her for sometime.

46

My husband and I

The next morning she said, "I've got a request I want you to pray about. I'm having a terrible time with my back. I want you to pray that the Lord will show you why I'm suffering." Now this kind of request was familiar to me. When I was growing up, my mother used to say when she was sick, "You don't have to pray for my healing; just pray for the Lord to reveal why He is chastening me, and when I obey I'll be healed." I don't hear these kind of requests very much this day and time. Jesus is the same yesterday, today, and forever.

Aunt Adelia and I started praying. The Spirit of the Lord began to work, and the Holy Ghost moved on me to lay hands on her. When I did, I said, "It's tithes and you used it."

She stopped praying and said, "That's it. I owed Brother Jones ten dollars tithes here a while back, and I used the money to buy something, but I intended to pay it back." This was over fifty years ago. Money wasn't as plentiful as it is today. She called her son Brother George Murray who was about ten or twelve years old at the time and told him, "You go to the barn and shell enough corn to sell for ten dollars." Well, what do you know, another miracle! She was healed.

Years ago Sister Tullos, who was in the church here, used to say, "When you get sick, search for the reason. Look under every little chunk." I know sometimes God is trying to get some little foxes out of our lives.

Again the Lord led me to Jigger,

My husband (A.O. Holmes)

Louisiana, for a few nights. Back in those days, since people in the country didn't have telephones, many times pastors did not know beforehand that a preacher was coming. This was one of those occasions. I caught a bus one night so I would arrive in daylight. I'll never forget that night; Brother Holmes said, "I hate to see you go with no one to meet you." The church was six miles from where I would get off the bus. I asked, "Would you send one of your children somewhere and not have someone to meet them?"

I got really sick before the bus got to Pine Bluff, and I was sick all the way; I felt like I had the flu. The next morning I got off the bus at seven o'clock in the little town of Jigger. The bus station was in a department store. I asked a clerk there if I could leave my suitcase and pick it up later and she agreed. I started walking out of town down the gravel road toward the home of the pastor, Brother Jones, but before I got out of the city limits, I saw a car approaching. It was Sister Roberson from Brother Jones's church. She stopped and asked, "Is that you, Sister Holmes? Where are you going?" When I told her she said, "Get in. I'm going to Winnsboro, and then I'll take you where you want to go."

I was happy to get in. We picked up my suitcase and were on our way. I tried to keep Sister Roberson from knowing how sick I was. She evidently had a lot of shopping to do and someone to visit in the hospital, so it was late in the evening before we left Winnsboro. I was too sick to shop, so I sat in her car all day. When we started home, she said, "Sister Holmes, do you want me to take you to Brother Jones's house? I'd rather take you home with me; you can go to church from my house."

I said, "That will be fine." I felt the same way I had riding on the bus; "I'm so sick; if I can just get off this bus!" Now I thought, "If I can just get out of this car!" What my tired body desired so much was a bed. When we got into her house, it was almost time to go to church. I said, "Sister Roberson, will you pray for me?" When she prayed, the Lord instantly healed me!

Soon we were riding down a country road to the church. I told the pastor, "The Lord has led me to come." He said, "Fine, Sister Holmes; we'll start a revival." I never had to worry when the Holy Ghost said, "Go!" I could be assured that when I got there another evangelist would not already be in revival. The Lord never gets crossed up.

The Lord blessed and we had a wonderful service with an amazing occurrence before the service was over. My mother, who lived in Bude, Mississippi, had a sister who lived about sixteen miles from Brother Jones's church. My aunt and her family went to another church called "Three Rivers." The Holy Ghost had spoken to my mother to catch a bus, go to her sister's house, and go to Three Rivers Church on Saturday night. I

Joel, Faith and I

My Mother and I

knew nothing about Mother's coming, and she knew nothing about my being in Louisiana.

Mother and my aunt went to church at Three Rivers, and on their way back to my aunt's home, they had to pass by Brother Jones's church. When they got within a mile of the church, the power of the Lord came upon my mother and she said, "I hate to ask this of you, but the Lord just spoke to me to stop at Brother Jack's church. I know it's late, but you can just sit in the car while I run in and see what the Lord wants." By this time George, my aunt's son, said, "Listen! That sounds like Sister Holmes's voice." They came in while I was preaching. I was so thrilled to see my mother that night; I had not seen her in many weeks. I was always glad to see her, but this was such a special time! I got my suitcase and went home with them. Mother's mission to Three Rivers was completed that night, so she joined us in the revival. God filled many souls with the Holy Ghost, and in about five nights I was back in Little Rock.

Jacksonville

One day sometime after the Lord had led us to North Little Rock, Brother Holmes said, "We are tired and need a break. Let's go to Hot Springs and rest for a few days." Sister Helen Russell, one of the teachers in our Christian school, who lived with us, kept our children.

Early the first morning after our arrival in Hot Springs, I woke up with a burden and started to pray. I remembered someone saying a few days earlier that Brother Hall, a minister who had visited our church a few times, had put up a tent in Jacksonville, which is ten miles from North

49

Little Rock. The tent, which was owned by the United Organizations, was made available to any member of that ministerial fellowship. Brother Hall was a member of this ministerial organization, but Brother Holmes did not belong to any organization.

While I was in the Spirit, the Lord made His will so clear to me that I could not doubt it. "I want you to go to Jacksonville and sit under the tent tonight," the Lord told me. We packed our clothes and headed back home. On the way, Brother Holmes said, "If you think you are going to preach under that tent, you are badly mistaken."

"I know that," I told him, "but all the Lord told me to do was to go and sit under the tent." I felt sorry for Brother Holmes because he had not gotten to rest, and I knew he felt sorry for me.

That night I went to the tent revival. After I sat down, I said, "Lord, here I am. What do you want?" After an outstanding young evangelist preached, there was a good response to the altar call. During the altar service, Brother Hall came over to me and told me that since the evangelist could not stay any longer, his plan was to take the tent down the next day unless I would be interested in preaching a few nights. I told him I would love to. I knew then why the Holy Ghost had sent me that night.

When I got home that night, Brother Holmes asked, "What happened?"

"I'm scheduled to preach tomorrow night under the tent," I replied.

Since Brother Hall was not pastoring a church, when the revival ended and the tent was taken down, the people began attending our church. Included in the group was a young couple, who later on was blessed with a baby boy. At an early age he exhibited great musical talent. He grew up to play the organ and went to college where he majored in music. What a blessing he has been to the church over the years, providing music in the church and teaching music in the school and church. Brother Tim Mullinax has deservedly been recognized as the best musician in the state.

Some time after this, Brother Brian Taylor was the pastor of a Pentecostal church in Jacksonville, Arkansas. While we held revival services, a young couple came one Sunday morning and again that night. The young man was stationed at the

My Mother

50

Little Rock Air Force Base. His wife was a Catholic and had never been to a Pentecostal church.

I preached about the Holy Ghost and how easy it is to receive. The young man came to the altar that night. He had never seen anyone go to the altar or receive the Holy Ghost. He knelt down, prayed a little bit, stood up and started jumping up as high as he could, raised his hands and said, "God, give it to me!" Then he said, "God, I said, give it to me!" I had never heard anyone talk to God like that. I felt a little afraid, but he was just exercising childlike faith. I had told him that God would give him the Holy Ghost and he wanted it! After the third or fourth jump, the power of the Lord fell on him, and he fell back, speaking in tongues, into the arms of the men who were praying with him. It was so wonderful! It reminded me of the Scripture in which the Lord said, " . . . command ye me (Isaiah 45:11)."

Kilburn

Mother never had a telephone in her house, but she had a line straight to Heaven. After my father passed away, she would catch a bus and come to see us. Once, as she packed her suitcase to come, she prayed, "Lord, send Wiley (her brother) to take me to the bus station."

Uncle Wiley was plowing in a little field behind his house, about a mile from Mother's. The Holy Ghost came upon him, and he began speaking in tongues. The Lord spoke, "Go to Ida (my mother); she needs you." Uncle Wiley tied the mule to a post, got into his car, and drove to Mother's. Looking in, as he walked up the steps, he saw Mother standing at the door. He asked, "What do you need?"

"I told the Lord to send you to take me to catch the bus," she replied. He did!

It was forty miles to Natchez where Mother had to change buses. As she waited there for the next bus, she went upstairs to the ladies' room. There the Holy Ghost fell on her and said, "Get off at Kilburn." She could not understand why since she didn't know anyone there, but she told the bus driver to let her off at Kilburn. There wasn't a bus station at Kilburn; tickets were purchased in the grocery store. The bus arrived there at nine o'clock that night. The store was closed, it was dark, and she was the only one to get off the bus.

Standing there in the dark with her suitcase as the bus drove away, she saw a light in the Pentecostal Church about a block away. She walked to the church and came in to find me behind the pulpit preaching. I was not expecting Mother to come to Little Rock, and she did not know that I was in Kilburn, which was one hundred fifty miles from Little Rock. I was so happy when she stepped inside that door and I saw her smiling face.

51

Had she not had that straight-line telephone from earth to Heaven, she would have passed right on through Kilburn, missed me, and arrived in Little Rock expecting to surprise us.

Biloxi

The Lord led me to Biloxi for a few nights' revival. Sister Jordan, a member of our church in North Little Rock, and my older son Ruebel, who was four years old at the time, had ridden there with me on a Greyhound bus. On the way home, we went by Bude to visit my parents for a few days. The morning after we arrived there, the Spirit of the Lord began to move as we prayed. The Lord showed me to go to Bethel Temple Church, which was ten miles from the bus station at Brookhaven. I called home and got Brother Holmes's permission to go. Since there were few telephones, I had to write the pastor a card to tell him how the Lord had spoken to me. Saturday morning I received his card telling me that the state presbyter of the United Pentecostal Church was beginning a revival that Saturday night, but he welcomed us to come and be in service with them.

I thought, "Lord, I don't understand this. I can't see myself traveling by bus, finding a way to get ten miles out to the church and taking Sister Jordan, my little boy, and me to their house with a minister already there."

I called Brother Holmes back and told him we would be leaving Mother's to catch the bus for Little Rock at twelve o'clock. A happy voice answered, "Come on!" I was happy, too. Although I had been gone but a few days, I was already homesick.

We had to change buses in Brookhaven with about an hour's wait. A burden fell on me while I was sitting in that little bus station; the longer I sat, the more burdened I felt. It was almost time to get on the bus, but I felt so burdened by the Holy Ghost. I thought, "I can't leave this town feeling like this."

Sister Jordan was so thrilled that we were going home. I thought, "How can I tell her, Lord? She will think I'm losing my mind." Finally, feeling the fear of the Lord, I got the courage to ask her, "Would you mind waiting and catching the six o'clock bus home? I can't get on this bus."

When the bus left I said, "Let's walk around and see if there are any Pentecostal people." I had become willing, even glad, to go to Bethel Temple for service that night, regardless of who was there, if we could only find a ride. We walked up and down the streets but saw no one that looked Pentecostal.

We went back to the bus station and sat for about four hours, waiting for the next bus. About twenty minutes before time to leave for Little Rock, I told Sister Jordan that I'd get something for Ruebel to eat on the bus since we would be on the road all night. As I was ordering a hamburger, someone walked up behind me, calling my name. Turning, I saw Brother Wilson, the pastor from Bethel Temple. "Sister Holmes," he said, "I have been to Bude looking for you. I have driven up and down these roads in a forty-mile radius for a week announcing this revival over a speaker on my car. Today I got a telegram from the preacher saying that he can't come. Would you please come?"

I said, "I'll have to call Brother Holmes and ask."

When I called and explained, Brother Holmes said, "You obey God." I'll never forget how I felt that Saturday night. The church was packed out; they were looking for someone really special, a great preacher. I felt as if I were about two inches tall, but knew I was in the perfect will of God. I thought, "This church will not be half full tomorrow night," but Sunday night, to my surprise, the church was full, and the crowd continued throughout the revival.

In a few days Brother Holmes came and helped us in the revival. I remember asking Sister Jordan the day Brother Holmes called to tell me he was coming, "Sister Jordan, will you be glad to see Brother Holmes, too?" I knew that by this time she was very homesick.

"Sister Holmes," she exclaimed, "I'd be glad to see a cat from Little Rock!"

Sister Marilyn Smith was with me in a revival at Brother James Springer's church in Biloxi, Mississippi. There was a real move of the Spirit. Attending services was a Baptist minister who was stationed at Keesler Air Base. One night he came forward after the service and told us that he had a prayer request. He said, "I want you to pray for my commanding officer. He is such a wicked person; he uses the Lord's name in vain almost every breath." The next night he said, "My commanding officer has promised to come with me to church!" Sure enough, the next night he came; the first time he had ever been inside a Pentecostal church. That was the end of Brother Mackey's cussing!

Dressed in a striking uniform with stripes and buttons, he was a nice looking young man in his early twenties. The Lord knew just what to do. A spirit of conviction settled over the congregation. After a short sermon, he was the first one to the altar; tears rolling down his face as he cried out to God. The Baptist preacher joined the others who came to the altar to help pray. It was only minutes until the power of the Lord came upon Brother Mackey and he began to tremble and shake; then he stood to his feet and began shouting and speaking in other tongues! The Baptist preacher tried to hold him, but about then we all got the Holy Ghost over again— except for the Baptist preacher. He received the Holy Ghost a few nights later.

Later on God filled Brother Mackey's wife with the Holy Ghost. The Lord called him to preach and they remained faithful to the Biloxi Church until he completed his enlistment in the Air Force. Brother Mackey now pastors a Pentecostal church near Chicago.

A Healing Touch

When Sharon was born, we lived at 2323 East Second Street. The weather was bad — cold and raining a lot; icicles hung from the eaves of the house for about three weeks. I became really sick and depressed. Brother Holmes and the entire church prayed for me, but it seemed I just grew weaker and weaker. As I stood in the bedroom one morning, I began trembling from head to toe. I decided that there was no use to fight any longer. Although I dreaded very much to die and leave my little baby, Brother Holmes, and the rest of the children, I had suffered with an affliction in my body so long it seemed I was at the last mile.

Brother Holmes said, "I'm going to call your mother to come." He called her that evening, but she couldn't leave before the next morning. As she packed her suitcase, she began praying, and since she lived alone, she could pray undisturbed most of the night. She caught the bus early the next morning and arrived in Little Rock that afternoon. When she arrived at our house, she walked straight to the bedroom where I was resting. As she entered the room she said, "You are not going to die. I sought the Lord last night and at three o'clock this morning I asked Him, Lord, are you going to take Agnes? He said, No, she can work in my vineyard. So you are going to be all right." Her face looked like an angel's face to me, and there was something about her hands when she pressed them on my brow that felt different from any other hands. The Lord did not completely heal me right then, but it seemed like a beacon of sunshine began shining in our house.

There was a revival at the Crystal Hill Pentecostal Church, which was pastored by Sister Jordan. Brother Holmes suggested, "Let's drive out to Crystal Hill to the revival tonight."

"You go. I just don't feel like it," I replied.

"Come on, you might feel better," he urged. Mother helped me get ready and we all went.

The small church was packed with people. I remember we found a seat about midway in the church. During the service that night the voice of the Lord spoke to me, "You are going to walk and not faint; you are going to run and not be weary." I came home feeling much better than when I went. In fact, from that very night I had new strength.

Revival at Home

There was a service somewhere almost every night. If we weren't in revival in the home church, we were driving back and forth preaching a revival somewhere else. This particular time we were in revival at the church. I had finished with the afternoon meal, and I thought about a lot of mending I needed to do. I had gathered the children's clothes that needed attention, hoping to find time to mend them. Then I thought, "I need to pray for the service tonight." I decided to go out to the church, which was only a few steps from our house, and pray. I entered the building and went through two or three Sunday school rooms and knelt to pray. I told the Lord in a low voice, "Lord, you are able to do so many things. I'll just ask you to patch and mend those clothes." I would have been embarrassed for anyone to hear me ask the Lord to patch. I continued in prayer. When I finished, I knew it was time to begin getting ready for church. When I opened the door of the church to walk home, I saw one of the ladies from the church sitting on the steps. I said, "Hello, Sister Hattie. You are early for church."

"I came early to see if you had any mending or patching you needed done," she said. I was so shocked. I had not expected the Lord to get started on it so soon!

One morning after the children had gone to school and as Brother Holmes was leaving to go to the church, he asked, "Mother, what about your baking us a banana cake today?" I said, "All right," remembering that I also had some ironing to do. I looked at the clock and said to myself, "I'll pray for thirty minutes before I start ironing." It seemed a battle to pray, like there was a wall, until about the last of the thirty minutes. Then, as I began to feel the Spirit making intercession, I thought it would be foolish to get up. I looked at the clock and purposed to pray thirty more minutes. Well, by the end of that thirty minutes, I didn't want to stop. I thought, "Oh, I can iron fast, I'll just get back down to the stream and drink for another hour." That hour went by so quickly, I decided, "This is too wonderful to stop now. One more hour, Lord."

The power of the Lord became so strong in the room, I said, "Lord, I'm not doing well. This is a day of good tidings. Lord, I feel like running out into the street and finding someone to tell how wonderful you are." I didn't know which way to go. Then I began praying, "Lord, send someone to my home. Let me share some of this with them."

In a few minutes the Spirit seemed to lift, so I got my ironing board out. As I began ironing the first garment, the doorbell rang. I went to the door, and there stood a neighbor of mine. I invited her in and thought, "Could this be the one God has sent?" She was about seventy years old and weighed about ninety-eight pounds. Puzzled, I asked her, "Have you received the Holy Ghost?"

She replied, "No."

I went on, "Well, do you realize if Jesus should come or call you away, you would be lost? The Bible says you must be born again of the water and the Spirit."

She asked, "Sister Holmes, do you have time to pray with me?"

I turned the iron off and said, "Get on your knees and start calling on the Lord. If you have hatred in your heart against anyone or owe anyone any money which you don't intend to repay, or if you dip snuff, you can't get it."

She looked right straight at me and said, "I love everybody; I don't dip snuff, and I don't owe a nickel in the world."

I told her joyfully, "Well, you can get it!"

She closed her eyes and lifted her voice to Heaven. At first her voice sounded weak, but all at once it sounded like she had been plugged into an electric amplifier. She began to shake under the power of the Lord and to speak in other tongues as the Spirit of the Lord gave the utterance. A smile came on her face, and we had a wonderful time together.

When she got through rejoicing and left, it was getting late. I remembered I had promised Brother Holmes a banana cake. Still so happy, I put the ironing into the freezer, and I said, "Lord, I'll bake this cake if you won't leave me." I cooked supper and baked the cake before my family arrived home for supper. After they finished eating, I brought the dessert. Brother Holmes said, "Mother, that banana cake doesn't look like the ones you've been baking." I said, "Well, I baked it in the Spirit." Brother Joel, who was about fourteen years old then, said, "Well, we may have to get in the Spirit to eat it!"

Sister Adams

Sister Adams's husband was in a branch of the military and was transferred to the Little Rock Air Force Base at Jacksonville. When the time came for their move to Jacksonville, Sister Adams went to visit her mother while her husband came on here. A short distance from her mother's home, there was a tent revival in progress. She went one night and received the baptism of the Holy Ghost. When she joined her husband in Jacksonville, she was a different person than she was when he left, and he really didn't like it; all her makeup was gone.

One night after service Sister Adams came to us with an urgent prayer request. She said, "Sister Holmes, I'm going through a trial." She began telling about how her Air Force husband's friend would come over to visit him and they would drink some and play cards. They would make fun of her and call her a "Holy Roller." She said, "At first it didn't seem to bother me, but here lately it's getting to me." I saw it was serious, and I immediately thought of the scripture, "If two of you shall agree on earth as touching any thing that they shall ask, it shall be done for them (Matthew 18:19)." I said, "Sister Adams, you and I are going to agree and pray and God will intervene. There is no playhouse the Devil builds that God can't tear up!"

The next service or two later, she came back to me and said, "They were carrying on the other night and I told them that they were such big cowards, they were afraid to come to church with me. This Air Force officer said that he'd come, and my husband spoke up and said that he'd keep our children (three little boys) if his friend would go with me!" She added, "He said that the only way he would come was if I'd sit by him at church. I didn't know what to tell him."

I assured her, "Yes, tell him you'll sit with him."

Sunday night came. Mr. Adams, true to his word, babysat. This officer, who weighed about two hundred pounds, was about thirty-five years old. He wore his uniform with all those stripes and stars. When they got to the door, he almost turned back, but Sister Adams said, "I knew you would chicken out!" That did it. He came on in, and they sat about midway of the congregation. Everyone except Brother Holmes and me thought Sister Adams has brought her husband. It was the usual great Sunday night service. I remember praying under my breath, "Lord, this is your night; this is your opportunity. There he sits God. Get him!"

Brother Holmes and I were sitting on a small pew on the platform. He leaned over and asked if I felt a message on my heart. I nodded, "I believe I do." It was a little simple message, not very long, but we felt the anointing of the Lord. I felt the words the Holy Ghost gave me were directly to him. While I was delivering my soul, I noticed he was moving closer to the edge of the pew. When the altar call was given, he was the first man to the altar. He didn't know how to kneel at the altar; he just fell on his knees in front of the pulpit. In a flood of tears with crying and repentance, he called out to the Lord with all his might. The brethren gathered around him, and in a short time he was brimming full of the Holy Ghost. By the time he finished rejoicing and Brother Holmes had baptized him, the service had continued a little longer than usual. That airman left that service a new creature in Christ Jesus.

Sister Adams said to herself, "I'm going to let him tell it." When they got home and rang the doorbell, Mr. Adams greeted them with a question, "Where have you guys been?"

The officer exclaimed, "I got the Holy Ghost!"

"I don't believe it!" exclaimed Mr. Adams

Then Mr. Adams asked his wife, "Did he really?" She assured him, "He really did!" Well, that ended the persecution at her house. The scripture is so true! "Ask and you shall receive."

The last time I saw that officer, he was still living for the Lord. The Holy Ghost makes new creatures of us. And I'm so happy to report that years on down the road, Brother Adams received the Holy Ghost.

Chapter 12

✝

A Little Boy with a Burden

When Brother Joel was just a baby, six months old, he would start leaping in my arms when the music began in church. Sister Lucas, a saint in the church, would say, "There is your preacher right there." When he was about three years old, he would say, "When I'm grown, I'm going to pray for the sick." One night Sister Gardner was sitting in her usual seat on the second pew. Brother Joel went over to speak to her. When she showed him how one of her ankles was swollen, he just dropped down on his knees, put his hands on her ankle, and prayed for her.

When he was five years old, he came to me one evening while I was cooking supper and said, "Mama, will you pray with me to get the Holy Ghost?" I said, "Yes, but let me finish what I'm doing." He went away for a few minutes, but came back, asking again, "Will you pray with me? I want the Holy Ghost!" I then realized that he was under conviction so I walked into the living room with him and sat down on the couch. He started weeping and praying, and the next thing, he began speaking in tongues and rejoicing. He was filled with the Holy Ghost!

Always when one of the family was sick, he had such compassion. When he was about eight years old, I was going through a terrible trial with bursitis in my arm and shoulder. During my suffering he would stay right by my side for hours, rubbing my arm and praying. I'd say, "Joel, don't you want to go outside and play?" If he went, he would only stay away a short time; then he would be back right by my side.

When we lived in Biloxi the second time, we started to Arkansas on a visit. We stopped by Bude to visit my parents, and Brother Holmes had an attack of kidney stones. He said, "There's no way I can go on to Little Rock." Brother Joel got down on his knees and started praying and didn't stop until his daddy was free from pain and we were able to go on to Arkansas. Little did we know that some day he would fill his father's shoes and be so mightily used of God.

When Brother Joel was twelve years old, Brother Lucas gave him a job in his produce market on Saturdays. Later he got a job working at a drug store on the same block in which we lived. It was near Christmas and the first things he bought were an electric razor for his daddy and a gift for me. It was the first electric razor Brother Holmes had ever owned. It seemed like Brother Joel was always thinking of others rather than himself.

When we would go to Mississippi to visit my family, Faith would always take one of her dolls for Mother to make a new doll dress. One particular time Joel thought, "What's wrong with all Faith's dolls having a new dress?" He was two-and-a-half years older than Faith, and he knew I wouldn't let her take more than one doll, so he helped her hide all her dolls under a quilt which they spread across their knees in the back seat. When we saw both children sitting so quietly in the back seat of the car waiting to leave, we knew something was amiss and discovered the dolls.

Joel and I

Faith, Joel, and Ruebel Holmes

60

Chapter 13

A Pillar in the Church

"Even a child is known by his doings, whether his work be pure, and whether it be right" (Proverbs 20). God not only uses adult saints to make a strong church, but He also uses dedicated young people. They can be great examples to the world of how the Lord can work even in the life of a child.

Donnie Lucas was one whose light shone brightly in his short life span. His parents were very faithful saints in our church. Donnie received the baptism of the Holy Ghost and was baptized in the name of Jesus at a very early age. He began working at the produce market with his father after school and on Saturdays. Since he was such a good worker, he made forty dollars a week, which was a good wage for a young boy back in the late fifties.

Donnie was faithful to church and worship. He never failed to put his tithes in an envelope, writing "Donnie Lucas - $4.00," and dropping it into the offering plate. I'll never forget the last Sunday night he was at church. Since he had helped his father unload produce until about two o'clock that Sunday morning, Brother and Sister Lucas did not wake him up to go to Sunday school with them. That Sunday night he came to Brother Holmes, his pastor, and said, "I want to apologize for not being at church this morning." He was only fifteen years old, but what a saint!

That night he sang in the choir and worshipped the Lord, dancing in the Spirit. It seemed like he was blessed more than usual. Someone made the remark, "I wish you would look at Donnie." He was so happy in the Holy Ghost.

The following Monday night we had to attend a fellowship meeting in Hot Springs. The young people's leader took a group of young people that morning for an outing before the scheduled service. Brother Holmes and I went early in the afternoon to Lake Hamilton where, as we approached, a group of the young people came running to the car. I cried, "Brother Holmes, something is wrong!" One of the young people exclaimed, "Donnie is under the water, and he has been down too long." By the time we could get out of the car, the rescue squad was carrying his body to the dock.

It was a sad time; his family was devastated. The whole church felt such loss. I'll never forget how for days I felt such grief. Then one day I was cleaning the living room thinking about what a precious saint of God our church had lost, when God dropped these words in my heart:

Little Donnie

It was on one bright cool morning when a group went out for the day,
Not thinking upon their returning that one would be called away.
As they rode down the highway that morning, everyone so jolly and gay,
Not dreaming that Heaven was calling for Donnie to come fill his place.
We miss you little Donnie. We miss you since Jesus took you away.
We know that in Heaven you are happy, with God and the angels to stay.
You have left your loved ones and friends behind; you have gone to treasures untold.
You'll live in a city called Heaven, where streets are made with gold.
You'll sit down by the river that flows from God; you'll walk in paths angels have trod.
You'll lean on walls of jasper grand, while gazing at beauties not made by hands.
Your smiles will be missed at the market. Your smiles will be missed in the school.
Your smiles will be missed in the home, Dear. Your smiles will be missed in the pew.

As I sat there singing those words, God took the grief from my heart. I know beyond any doubt that Donnie, whom God made a pillar in our church for just a short time, is standing somewhere around the grandstand in Heaven today enjoying that beautiful City.

Chapter 14

The Stroke

Brother Holmes had such a burden for souls. He had the work of God at heart and burned the candle at both ends; late to bed but early to rise was his normal routine. He never cared to hunt or fish, or even to take a vacation. His idea of a vacation was to attend a camp meeting somewhere, or to preach a revival away from home.

I'll never forget the day he had the stroke. Early that morning on Good Friday, April, 1969, he received a telephone call to come to the Baptist Hospital and pray for a lady there, who was dying with cancer. Brother Holmes asked a young man, who was living in our home and teaching in the Christian school, to drive us to the hospital.

He made the visit and prayed. We left the hospital room, and as we were riding down in the elevator, Brother Holmes said, "I don't feel good." By the time we reached the hospital door, he said, "I feel like I can't stand up."

The young man cried, "I'll run and get the car." It looked as if Brother Holmes would fall on the sidewalk where we were waiting. I was praying, "Lord, help us!" When the car arrived, Brother Holmes walked over and got in. Those were the last steps he ever took alone. When we drove under the carport at home, we had to help him out of the car and into the house to bed.

This was the greatest trial we had ever faced since we had been married. The saints began to gather into our home to pray. Preachers came from far and near. Someone said, "You need to get a hospital bed." I thought, "Oh, no! We don't need a hospital bed. God will heal him, and he'll be walking and normal again." Prayer went up for him everywhere, but somehow the Lord did not see fit to heal his paralyzed body.

Brother Joel, then nineteen years old, was evangelizing. He came home and began taking care of the church. The Lord was so real to us all the way through this terrible time. After a few days Brother Holmes could be taken back to church. From that, we began to go out for revivals. It was miraculous the revivals God gave us with thirty and forty receiving the Holy Ghost.

My husband, A. O. Holmes, and I

Juanita and Terril with their grandchildren

Juanita and Terril Beall

David and Kristen Beall with Madeline and Bram

Rev. Johnny Hair and Lyndal with their children and grandchildren

Todd and Sherry Davis,
Allen, Dana, and Jonathan

Leland, Carol, Jennifer and Loren Dyson

Todd and Sherry Davis with their children Dana, Jonathan, and Allen

Carol Dyson with her children Loren and Jennifer

Rev. Joe Burgess and Robin with their children Blake and Brooklyn

David and Kristen Beall, Madeline and Bram   *Blake and Brooklyn Burgess and Juliana Hair*

Jon and Julie Hair

Calvin Smith with his children and grandchildren

Cal and Lisa Smith, Laura and Callie

Candy Smith

Terry and Cathy Coffman, Leslie and Arlie

Laura and Callie Smith

Leslie Coffman

Leslie's graduation
Sis. Holmes, Juanita and Arlene

Cal, Candy and Cathy with Callie

Vaiden and Karen Holmes, Kelli, Trey, Kaci and Vaiden Joseph

David and Shelia Harrison and Candice

Granddaughter Shelia Harrison and Sis. Holmes

Vaiden and Karen Holmes, Trey, Kaci and Vaiden Joseph

Sheila Harrison, Candice and Ashley

Vaiden Joseph and Kaci Holmes

Holmes Family at Nathan and Mandie's wedding reception in North Little Rock

Pastor and Sister Holmes; Nathan and Mandie Holmes;
Roger, Andrea and Cydney Cypert

Mandie and Nathan Holmes

Holmes Family at wedding of Andrea and Roger Cypert

Sis. Holmes and granddaughter Andrea Holmes at her wedding

Sis. Holmes and great-granddaughter, Cydney

Faith, Chelsea and Nicole Cavin

Nicole Cavin

Chuck, Faith, Chelsea and Nicole Cavin

Nicole Cavin   *Chelsea Cavin*

The Brewer Family – Ronnie, Sharon Rose, Justin, Brittany, Renee and Joey

Joey, Renee and Justin Brewer

Brittany and Joey Brewer

Joey and Justin Brewer

Juanita Beall, Faith Cavin, Rev. J. N. Holmes, Sharon Brewer, Sis. Holmes and Ruebel Holmes

Sis. Holmes and her grandchildren

Sis. Holmes and her great-grandchildren

Sis. Holmes and her great-great-grandchildren

Sis. Holmes and Ruebel   *Sis. Holmes and Joel*

Sis. Holmes and Faith   *Sis. Holmes and Sharon*

Sis. Holmes and Janet

(Standing L to R) – Sharon, Juanita, Faith;
(Seated L to R) – Ruebel, Sis. Holmes, Joel

Varden, Sis. Holmes and Ruebel

(L to R) Jan Holmes, Andrea, Sharon, Faith,
Chelsea, Sis. Holmes and Renee

Sis. Holmes with Andrea, Nathan, Nicole, Justin and Joey

Chelsea Cavin and Renee Brewer

Nathan, Andrea and Joey

Sis. Holmes with Nathan and Joey

Sis. Holmes, her brother Bernette Clark and her sister Jimmie Ross

(L to R) Linda, Pauline, Bernette, Ricky

Sis. Holmes's sister Jimmie Ruth Ross

(L to R) Layla, Teddy, Tylina, Alex, Leonard and Lyndel

(L to R) Damon Clark, Pauline, Bernette, Tylina

*(L to R) Jimmie Ruth, Sis. Holmes, her nephew Randy Alexander
and his wife Debra*

(L to R) Sis. Holmes's husband Bishop A. O. Holmes, Ollie, Lexie and Roy

(Standing L to R) Danny, Sis. Holmes, Faith, Ronnie
Bishop A. O. Holmes in wheelchair

Larry Wilson
Adopted Son

Danny Walters
Adopted Son

Sis. Holmes and Sis. Morar

Sis. Holmes with cousin Grace Lee
in Meadville, MS

Rev. Jerry Cox, Sis. Holmes, Faith and Sharon

Bro. Joel, Sis. Alnita Gill and Sis. Holmes

Faith, Sis. Holmes and her sister, Jimmie Ruth Ross

Sis. Holmes and Sis. Brockinton
on their way to Europe

Bro. Joel, Sis. Holmes and Renee

Sis. Holmes, Sis. Jan Yeats and Renee

(L to R) Rev. and Sis. Burr, Sis. Holmes, Sis. Toole, Megan Davies, Mandie, Nathan, Rev. and Sis. Davies

Sis. Holmes and Sis. Burr

Marty, Jimmie and Joel

Sis. Holmes, Renee, Sis. Singletary and Juanita

Chapter 15

Evangelizing after the Stroke

After Brother Holmes began feeling better, he wanted to go and visit his sister, Lexie, who lived in Buris, Louisiana. Faith and Sharon went with us. We stopped in Vidalia, Louisiana, on Saturday night to be in service with a cousin of mine, Brother George Murray. That night there was a mighty move of the Lord in the service. Brother Holmes still had such a burden to work for God that he asked Brother George if we could have a few nights service. Brother George said, "Sure, Brother Holmes; I'd be thrilled!"

We had a good revival in the next few nights, then we went on to Brother Holmes's sister's home in Buris. Her husband was pastoring a church there and asked us to preach a revival. That's the way we got started evangelizing after Brother Holmes was paralyzed.

Next, the Lord led us to Biloxi, Mississippi, to preach for Brother James Springer. Over forty souls received the Holy Ghost, including Brother Craig Sissel and his wife. Brother Sanford also prayed through during this revival. He lived at Seminary, Mississippi, where he was a member of the Baptist church. While visiting some family members who lived in Biloxi, he attended the revival. He received the Holy Ghost, got baptized in Jesus' name, and felt the call to preach. Not long after he got back to Seminary, the Baptist church asked him to preach some for them since the church was without a pastor at the time. Most everyone prayed until they received the Holy Ghost with the evidence of speaking in tongues and got baptized over in the name of Jesus. The church became a Pentecostal church and that's been over twenty years ago. He is still the pastor.

I can't find words to express how wonderful that revival in Biloxi was. It lasted five or six weeks with no rest nights.

After a revival, we were always glad to head back to North Little Rock. One day I was at the church praying and the Lord revealed to me it was His will for us to go to Brother Travis's church, but when I got home I thought, "What if I just thought that?" So I didn't call. A few days passed. I was in the Spirit and the Holy Ghost moved on my soul again. I said, "Lord, I promise I will call." When I called and said, "Hello," before I had time to tell who I was, Brother Travis said, "Is that you, Sister Holmes? If I had obeyed the Lord, I would have called you three days ago." He encouraged, "Come on, we are ready for revival." We packed the motor home and went.

Brother Albert Travis pastored the Sunny Hill Pentecostal Church in Sunny Hill, Mississippi, about six miles from any little town. We started in a revival there on a Sunday night. The Lord gave me a message about Zaccheus. Jesus came up to the tree and said, " . . . Zacchaeus, make haste, and come down; for to day I must abide at thy house" (Luke 19:5). I gave the altar call and five adults came to the altar. I was especially led to this one person. I started praying with this man, who, unknown to me, had been going to the altar for twenty-five to thirty years! The Devil zeroed in on him and said, "You won't feel a thing." Something told him, "You've been seeking a long time; why don't you do just what she says?" In a very short time, he received the Holy Ghost. Thirty-one people received the Holy Ghost in that revival.

One night a lady came who had never been to a Pentecostal church before. She got under conviction and received the Holy Ghost. At this time she and her husband were living with her mother. Her husband was working in New Orleans and came home on weekends. When he came home, he was so angry that she had gone to a Pentecostal church. One night during song service she was sitting on the second pew from the front when her husband came down the aisle and sat down by her. He said, "You come home *now!*" He was so angry. Right after he walked out, a victory march was started. In the victory march, this sister said to me, "Sister Holmes, my husband has demanded that I leave now. What must I do?"

I said, "No, don't leave. Stay until church is over."

When he returned to her mother's home, he started talking to her

My husband and I

66

mother about how upset he was. Although her mother didn't like the church either, it angered her that he would speak so harshly about her daughter, so she told him, "This is my house and if you don't like what she's doing, just get out; leave now!" He sat down on the couch and started crying. About this time his wife walked in. Her mother was so sorry for the way he was acting, she said, "I'll go to church with you tomorrow night." She did and received the Holy Ghost!

Each place we went was different. We enjoyed them all. I'll never forget the first night of a particular revival. The motor home was parked close to the church. As he always did, Brother Holmes had us help him get into the church early. After a little while, he sent someone to tell Faith and Sharon to bring their horns.

We walked into the church to find Brother Holmes so amused. We soon understood the cause of his amusement. The woman at the piano was past eighty. Don't misunderstand; she was doing a good job of playing. There stood a sister in her sixties with her hair in a ponytail beating the drum. The guitar player was an elderly man who lived in a rest home, and had been brought by one of the saints. And there we were: Brother Holmes in a wheelchair, I past my young days, and Sharon and Faith feeling their limitations. We were all amused; it was so different from what we were accustomed to. But we loved it!

My husband and I in the motor home

We saw the Scripture fulfilled, "Not by might, nor by power, but by my Spirit, saith the Lord of hosts" (Zechariah 4:6). God blessed every night and sent an outstanding revival. I remember the pastor requesting, "Pray a special prayer for my daughter who has been backslid for twenty years. She and her family come to church every Sunday. Sure enough, she was there that Sunday morning, and the Lord anointed. After service the pastor asked me what I thought about her. I confidently exclaimed, "I believe the Holy Ghost got her today!" Sure enough she and her children were back for service that night. She went to the altar and was filled with the Holy Ghost. Before the revival ended, her teenage daughter was also filled with the Holy Ghost.

Brother Holmes enjoyed his own little joke when we would be in revival with the Springers in Biloxi, Mississippi. Years before, while pastoring there, Brother Holmes had won the Whitehead family to the Lord. Their daughters had grown up and married, one to a boy named Pigg, the other to a boy named Fox. Each time these couples attended church, Brother Holmes loved to get the microphone and say, "We are glad to have the Piggs and Foxes here with us tonight." I would always cringe inside, but Brother Holmes would be grinning happily. I had no need to fear; it seemed he could get by with anything.

Once, when we were in revival with Brother and Sister Parker in Escatawpa, Mississippi, an elderly widowed preacher asked Brother Holmes for Mother's address. He explained that once while his wife was still living Mother had been with them in a street service, and he forgot to share the offering with her. Although this had occurred sometime before, he still wanted to send Mother some money.

Mother came the next day to be with us in revival. In the motor home that evening, Brother Holmes was sitting there in his wheelchair, and Mother was getting ready for church when she asked me, "Agnes, see if you can fix my hair." Brother Holmes began laughing and teased, "It's because Brother Ritchey (the widowed preacher) is coming!" He carried Mother high, continuing, "As long as I've been married to your daughter, I've never known you to ask her to fix your hair." My mother was trying desperately to tell him that no thought of such a thing was in her mind.

Daddy had passed away when Mother was sixty-four, and she was now past seventy. After Daddy's passing, she always said that she wasn't going to act like a goose and let some man nail her feet to the floor. She explained that in bygone times this was the method of fattening a goose to bake for family dinner. The feet of the goose were nailed to the floor and corn was placed in front of him. He could eat, but he couldn't move around and run the fat off.

As soon as we arrived at church that night, Brother Holmes began telling some of the young people that he been teasing Mother about the widower. Mother prayed God wouldn't let him come that night. Sure enough, he failed to show up!

During the time we were evangelizing, after preaching a revival in Jonesboro, Georgia, with Brother and Sister Jack Ollis, we went to New Orleans to be with Sister Lois Gatlin. Since we were starting the revival that night, I went out to the church to pray as soon as we arrived. As I walked to the church, I thought, "I wish we had a car so that we could get out of the motor home and just ride for awhile." After living in a motor home for a few weeks, the walls seemed to move in closer. As I prayed I said, "Lord, I'm going to ask you in Jesus' name to provide a car." I didn't want Sister Gatlin to know about my prayer request since she had several children and was always so busy. When I finished praying for the service that night, I went back to the motor home where Brother Holmes and Faith were. Just minutes later a young man drove up, parked his car, and knocked on our door. Brother Holmes, in his normal friendly way, invited him in, although we had never met him before. He said, "I am a member of this church." After a little while he said, "I must go so that I can get back for service tonight." Then to my great surprise, he asked, "How would you folks like for me to come tomorrow and just drive you all around over New Orleans? I've lived here for years, and I know this city well." He took three pictures from his pocket, each one of a limousine! He continued, "I can come for you in a gold limousine, a black limousine, or a white limousine.

Brother Holmes exclaimed, "That will be great!"

The young man invited, "Just name the time."

Sister Terrell, my Mother, and I

Brother Holmes answered, "Around nine o'clock will be fine."

I stood there open-mouthed, thinking, "Before morning I'll have to check this out." I asked Sister Gatlin, the pastor, "What about this young man?"

"He's all right," said Sister Gatlin.

"What about the cars?" I asked.

"He and his father come to church sometimes in a gold limousine, sometimes in a white limousine, and sometimes in a black limousine."

The young man was right on time the next morning. He helped Brother Holmes into the front seat of the limousine. Faith and I were seated way back in the back seat. The sun shone beautifully as we rode in the luxurious car around the city. I thought, "Lord, you beat anything I've ever seen! I would have been happy to ride in an old-model car, or even in a Volkswagon!"

When we returned home, Mother had came to visit us. During her visit we received a telephone call from Brother and Sister Dawson in California asking us to come to preach a "pre-camp" for a youth camp. We jumped at the opportunity. I had been to California, but my mother had never been and I thought she would love to see it. We told Sister Dawson yes without even praying about it.

The day before we were to leave I was packing for the trip, and every time I would put an article of clothing in the luggage something would say, "What's this title I see?" I thought, "Lord, is this you? What do you mean by this?" I didn't tell anyone about it.

That evening we were invited to eat supper with Brother Joel and Sister Jan. We planned to eat with them that evening, then leave early the next morning. On the way to their home, the power of the Lord came on my mother in the back seat of the car, and she started speaking in tongues. When the Spirit lifted, she said, "I can't go with you to California. The Lord just spoke to me and I can't go."

I thought, "Looks like we'll have to go on without her; we've already promised." Then I thought, "We really ought to pray about this, since the Holy Ghost is stopping her."

Christmas at Brother Joel and Siser Jan's house

When we got back home after eating that good supper, I began to pray and I became afraid. The Holy Ghost spoke to me saying, "Go to Pine Grove Church." Brother Jerome Bourn was pastoring the church at that time. (Brother Holmes used to pastor that church.)

There was a man in that church who went to the altar for forty years without receiving the Holy Ghost. He supported the church financially, paid his tithes and never missed going to the altar when an altar call was given, but it looked like he would die without the Holy Ghost. When Brother Holmes was pastoring the church, we'd have revivals and this man just wouldn't yield to the Spirit.

We called Brother Bourn and he said, "Come on!"

The first service, all I felt to preach was, "What's this title that I see?" There was a cemetery right behind the church. I told them about how we were all packed and ready to go to California and the Holy Ghost spoke to us to go to Pine Grove. I said, "I don't know if some of you are about to be placed in that cemetery behind the church or not. I don't know what it means but I know it's from God." That man received the Holy Ghost the next night! These words I didn't want to say scared him into yielding, and he got a wonderful experience with the Lord.

After this revival was over, we started preaching out in different places: Cato, Mayflower and other small communities close to North Little Rock.

Chapter 16

God Gives Faith a House

My daughter Faith was so inspired by the testimonies of different ones who had been blessed after giving sacrificially to the church that she decided to try the Lord. She was single, lived at home, and worked in an office in Little Rock. Her weekly take-home pay was about eighty dollars. Without telling anyone, she began dropping all her pay into the offering except enough for gasoline. She drove daily about twenty miles one-way. She continued this "giving her all" for a few times.

At that time we lived in the country seven miles from town. Along the route into town on four acres was a house that Faith had always noticed and admired, especially in the spring when the flowers were in bloom. One morning as she passed the house, it seemed the Lord brought to her mind the little sacrifice which she had been making. Faith gripped her heart, and she spoke the words, "Lord, give me that house!" Two or three other times as she passed the house, she repeated her prayer. She did not have one dollar to buy the house. No one but God knew about her desire. She did not breathe it to a living soul.

A few weeks passed. Then one day as she and I drove past the house, she exclaimed, "Oh, Mother! There's a 'For Sale by Owner' sign in that yard." She suggested we drive back so she could copy the phone number, but I discouraged her, saying, "Oh, Faith, that much land and a house this close to town would be so expensive."

"Probably so," she agreed, and we drove on.

Brother Joel lived a few miles away, nearer town. That day while he was at home, he felt an urge to drive over by the airport. From the airport he circled past our house, and on by the house Faith admired. The "For Sale" sign caught his eye; he stopped and made a note of the telephone number and hurried home to call. The lady who answered explained that the owner, who lived in New Jersey, had called her instructing her to put the house on the market and to ask $35,000 for it. She had just put the sign up about thirty minutes before. "Lady," said Brother Joel, "go out and take down your sign. I'll be right there with the earnest money." The next day another offer was made for more money if she would back out on Brother Joel. She refused.

A few days passed and then Brother Joel approached his sister. "Faith, I've been praying and wondering what to do with that place. How would you like for us to put in a daycare there? You run it and take half the profit."

"That sounds good," she replied.

"Then start checking into what we need to do to get started," he told her.

A few weeks after the day care had opened for business, Brother Joel told Faith, "I don't want to be involved in a day care business. You just go ahead with it. You can repay me for the down payment if you ever have it, but it is your place."

It was then that Faith told us the story of how as she passed the house, she had asked God for it. It wasn't long before she had made the money to pay Brother Joel what she owed him. The place proved to be a great blessing to her. God is so mighty! When you know Him, you need not always have the money to buy. Just have faith in God.

I was preaching a revival at Brother Cox's church in Pine, Louisiana, when I felt inspired to give this testimony. A few months later when I returned to the church, Sister Tally, a church member, walked over to me and said, "Sister Holmes, when you told about Sister Faith's house, I asked God to give *me* a house. Now, I have a house!"

Chapter 17

Aunt Jenny

It was early spring this special time that the Spirit led me to Brother and Sister Springer's in Biloxi, Mississippi, for revival.

About the second night, two sisters, Sister Sandra and Sister Kay, came up to me after service with a prayer request. They told me, "We have a great aunt whose name is Aunt Jenny. Our mother died when we were small children and Aunt Jenny has been a mother to us; we love her dearly. She now lives in a nursing home. She has never been to a Pentecostal church. A few days ago she became seriously ill with a kidney infection and double pneumonia. She was moved to the hospital at Gulfport where we have been sitting up with her. We love her so much, and she has never been saved. We feel she has been so kind to us that we can't stand to see her die lost. We are praying and believing that the Lord will touch her so she can come to this revival and receive the Holy Ghost and be baptized in the name of Jesus."

They came back the next night still praying and believing for Aunt Jenny. One night they were very excited. They had talked to her doctor that day and he promised that as soon as he could discontinue her IV, they could bring her.

A few more nights of the revival passed. Then one night I saw these two sisters, one on each side of a very weak elderly lady, whom they were assisting to walk. They sat down toward the back of the church. Since Aunt Jenny couldn't sit up, she lay over on one sister's shoulder.

Aunt Jenny didn't want to die without the Holy Ghost and being baptized in Jesus' name. When the altar call was given, some of us went back to pray with her. In spite of her weakness, she began to call on the name of Jesus. Soon the power of God touched Aunt Jenny, and she received the Holy Ghost with the evidence of speaking in other tongues.

We all came alive! A miracle had been performed before all our eyes. We could tell she was stronger when they helped her walk to the car that night.

The next night they brought her back to church. Aunt Jenny said she wanted to be baptized that night. It was March and the weather had turned cold. Brother Springer, who was away at the time, didn't have a baptistry. I nearly lost my faith. In my mind I could see them practically dragging Aunt Jenny along out into the almost ice cold water of the front beach — and her just recovering from double pneumonia.

I'll never forget how Brother Holmes, who was sitting there in that old wheel chair, spoke up and said, "Take her out to Brother Springer's house and baptize her in the bathtub." I thought, "Thank God for the answer."

As the revival continued on, Aunt Jenny got stronger and stronger. By the time the revival closed, Aunt Jenny was attending every night, could walk without help, and was as happy as she could be with her born-again-experience in the Lord. The revival ended and we went back to Little Rock.

A little over a year passed and we were invited to return to Biloxi for another revival. The first night in service I could hardly believe my eyes. When the choir was called up to sing, Aunt Jenny marched onto the platform to sing in the choir.

For several years, every time we were in Biloxi for revival, Aunt Jenny attended every service. She never went back to the rest home; one of the nieces took her into her home to live. When she was in her eighties, one day in August, just before time for camp meeting to begin in North Little Rock, I had a long distance call from the niece, Sister Sandra, with whom she lived. She was calling to tell me that she was bringing Aunt Jenny to camp meeting. I invited her to come to stay at my house.

I wondered the day they were to arrive if she would feel able to attend service that night after traveling almost five hundred miles. To my surprise, Aunt Jenny arrived eager to get to the church. It was beautiful to see her walking down the aisle; she began leaping and praising the Lord. I had prepared a meal for us to enjoy after church. As we were all seated, I looked at the clock and it was midnight. But there sat Aunt Jenny at the table with all of us eating, laughing, and talking. I thought, "Aunt Jenny, you are a living miracle."

Chapter 18

✝

Standing on the Highway

On a Wednesday after Brother Holmes and I had closed a revival in Florence, Mississippi (Sister Erma Jean Holland pastors that church today.), I was making preparations to leave for Magnolia to be in revival services there with Brother Jerry Terrell. I began to think since it was Wednesday that we might stop in McComb and attend mid-week services there with my cousin, Brother Jerome Bourn. There was time since revival at Brother Terrell's did not begin until Saturday night.

I prayed, "Lord if you want us to stop and be in service in McComb, you have Brother Bourn out on the freeway, and I'll know it's your will." As we drove down the freeway, I looked but saw no sign of Brother Bourn. I knew that he did not know that we were anywhere in Mississippi. I said, "Lord, I guess you don't want us to stop and be with them."

Since we needed gasoline, I exited off the freeway. I drove to a service station and stood in front of the motor home as the tank was being filled. About that time, Brother Bourn drove into the station. "Sister Holmes, where are you going?" he asked.

When I told him, this is what he said: "This brother I'm riding with is in our church. He called me this morning and said, 'Brother Bourn, I'm going down to Magnolia to buy my tag. Come ride with me and I'll buy your tag.' We drove the freeway there, but when we started back, the Holy Ghost spoke telling me to go home the old highway. I told the brother driving that I did not know why the Lord wanted us to go that way." He went on to say, "Sister Holmes, why don't you turn around and come preach my mid-week service?"

I was happy to do so. The Lord did not have him standing on the freeway, but he had me standing out on the old highway!

Chapter 19

✝

On My Own

After Brother Holmes went to be with the Lord, and Vaiden, my grand-son married, I was left alone. I felt so lonely because I was so used to being around people. Brother Holmes and I had raised six children of our own and there was always someone who needed a home, so we usually had someone else living with us as well. I never dreamed I'd be left in a big house alone. It was a different road than I had ever walked down, but God gave me grace. On the dresser in my bedroom was a picture of Brother Holmes. At night, if I turned on the light, that's the first place my eyes fell, and it seemed I could hear him say, "You must be so lonely here by yourself." After a few weeks I moved his picture to another place. I tried not to grieve even though I missed him very much. We had enjoyed so many wonderful years together. I began to realize that life has many changes. I really don't know how people make it without the wonderful baptism of the Holy Ghost, which is the Comforter.

It seemed like I was adjusting fairly well until one night I thought of a friend who had quit coming to church. I decided to call and invite her to church that weekend. When I started talking, I said a word or two and broke down crying and couldn't stop. She said, "What's wrong, Sister Holmes? Do you need something? Do you need me to come?" I finally regained my composure and apologized. After I had hung up, I felt all right so I decided to call Ruebel, my older son. After I had said a few worlds, the same thing happened again. He said, "Mother, what's wrong? What's happened?"

"I'm so sorry I cried," I replied, "I don't want you to feel bad."

While we were talking, the doorbell rang. Sister Angie Looper walked in and said, "We have some company at our house and some are sitting around playing checkers. I started thinking about you and decided to come over." She just lived a couple of miles down the road. In a few minutes, her husband came, also, and right after he sat down he said, "Sister Holmes, you ought to sell this house and move. You would be more satisfied."

"Do you really think so?" I asked.

About that time my telephone rang; it was my daughter, Sharon. She said, "Mama, I want you to come spend the night with me tonight."

I thought, "What's going on? It seems like everyone knows about this crying tonight." I said, "Sharon, did Ruebel call you?"

"No," she replied.

"Brother and Sister Looper are here with me," I told her.

She replied, "Mama, I'm not going to bed until you get here."

"Go, Sister Holmes," Brother Looper encouraged, "We'll follow you over there."

A few days later, Brother Joel called me from the church. It was service night and he was there fasting and praying for the service. He said, "Mother, let's build you a new house close to my house."

The first thing I thought was: "Brother Looper!" I asked, "Did Brother Junior Looper call you and say something about a house?"

"No," he replied.

I was still puzzled and asked, "Did Ruebel call you?"

He said, "No. No one has called me. I was praying today at the church, and the Lord impressed me to build you a new home."

I thought, "God, all I know is I must have sounded so pitiful to you that night when I burst out crying, you decided to move me into a beautiful new home."

Brother Joel and Sister Jan put beautiful furniture in this home which is just a short distance down the road from their house. Sharon and Faith live with their families in the next two houses. Brother Holmes didn't leave a lot of money but the Lord, through Brother Joel, has seen that I haven't lacked for anything.

Chapter 20

✝

On the Road Again

After Brother Holmes went to be with the Lord, I remembered the words he said before he left, "Mama, when the Lord takes me, don't you stop; go on working for the Lord."

I thought, "Lord, what do you want me to do?" I felt impressed to ask the Lord, "Lord, if you want me to preach a revival somewhere, send the pastor by and have him say, 'Come go home with us.'" God was the only one who knew I prayed that kind of prayer; I never told another living soul about my fleece. Only a few days had passed, when Brother and Sister Cox drove up to my house. They had been to Branson, Missouri. He said, "Sister Holmes, come preach for me. Just leave your car here and ride home with us." That's the way I got started back on the field. I was sixty-four years old at that time, and I've stayed busy ever since.

After I had preached the revival at Brother Cox's, I prayed, "Now Lord, you know I left my car at home. Wherever you lead me, I don't want anyone to make a special trip on my behalf."

I felt in the Holy Ghost to go preach for Brother and Sister Lott at Petals, Mississippi, around seventy miles away. I knew Brother and Sister Cox wouldn't mind taking me, but I asked God to do it for me. The revival at Brother Cox's closed. One of Brother Cox's daughters said, "Aunt Shirley (Sister Lott) is coming tomorrow night to a shower." It was arranged that I would go home with her. I thought, "Lord, this is just like I desired." God had planned that shower at the right time.

While I was preaching the revival at Brother Lott's church, Brother Joel called from North Little Rock and said, "Mama, we are coming to Brother and Sister Pullen's church for a special service. Do you want us to bring your car?"

I said, "Yes!"

Brother Pullen's church was only about thirty miles from where I was.

Chapter 21

Sister "Elijah"

I had closed the revival with Brother and Sister Lott in Petals, Louisiana, and feeling homesick to get back to Little Rock, was rushing about that Monday morning, packing my clothes. Thoughts ran through my mind of how I usually stopped at my cousin's house, Sister Erma Jean Holland, in Florence where she pastored a church. Sometimes I would spend the night with her. "But now," I thought, "she doesn't even know I am in the state. I just won't stop."

My cousin Rev. Jean Holland and I

The moment I had these thoughts, as I bent over to place something into my luggage, the Spirit of the Lord spoke, "And as often as he passed by, he went in and ate bread."

I said, "Now, Lord, are you telling me to stop by Sister Holland's?" I continued, "Lord, I will."

This was about 7:00 a.m., and I was about a hundred miles from her. I recalled that she always went to the bank on Monday, but I was afraid not to obey the Lord. When I drove up into her yard, she opened the door and said, "Come on in," and as I followed her, she added, "Don't sit down, come on to the table. We have just taken biscuits from the oven."

I began laughing as I sat down. I had to tell them how the Lord had spoken. The telephone rang, and Sister Holland answered the call from one of the saints in her church, "Come on over here. We have Sister Elijah with us this morning."

Well, I know I'm not worthy to be compared with the prophet Elijah, but I do know the God of Elijah!

Chapter 22

✝

Ministering Angels

To God be all the glory for every word of this book. Seeing and hearing angels does not make someone holier than any other child of God. Remember Cornelius in the tenth chapter of Acts. As he fasted and prayed before he received the Holy Ghost, an angel appeared unto him telling him to send to Joppa for Peter to come and tell him and his household words whereby they could be saved.

It was in the 1950's one Sunday night in the old church on the corner of Second and Buckeye Streets. I had completed a four-day fast. The power of God was falling like rain. At the end of the song service when everyone was going down from the platform to be seated, I felt the Spirit of the Lord so strong, that instead of sitting down, I walked across the church in front of the altar bench. When I reached the end of the altar, I turned around to see in a vision (my eyes were closed) over the altar, just out from the pulpit, an angel of the Lord. The appearance was from the waist up. His face was slightly larger than the face of a man and his hands were raised. There was a halo around his head, and a glow of the same color surrounded each finger.

It was so clear that I thought, "Everyone in the congregation must see this." I stood for a few seconds, not feeling the least bit afraid. I decided to approach the heavenly being, but when I had taken a step or two, the head faded away, leaving the arms and hands suspended for a second or two; then they just faded away, also.

My first words were, "Did you see the angel of the Lord?" Although it has been almost forty years ago, I have never forgotten that wonderful experience. The angel's appearance is still a vivid memory.

Many years later, after Brother Holmes had the stroke, we were evangelizing in Jonesboro, Georgia, with Brother and Sister Ollis. We were sleeping in the evangelist's quarters at the church when I suddenly awoke early one morning before dawn. I felt strongly impressed to get up and pray. The room was still dark, and I was so sleepy because we had gotten to bed quite late. I thought, "I believe I'll just go back to sleep."

It was then that I had the vision, this time with my eyes open. As clearly as could be, someone in a long, flowing robe as white as the light was slowly walking away from my bed, his head turned, looking back at me over his shoulder.

I called to Him, "Wait, Lord! I'm getting up."

Sometime after the Lord called Brother Holmes to be with Him, I received a telephone call from my cousin, Brother Larry Murray, who was pastor of a Pentecostal church in Meadville, Mississippi, inviting me to come for a revival. I accepted, since the Holy Ghost had been dealing with me about them. I enjoyed God's presence throughout the days there as well as in the services every night.

One day when Brother and Sister Murray were out visiting and I was alone in the parsonage, I felt rivers of the Holy Ghost flooding my soul. It was that indescribable fullness of joy, and I didn't want it to let up. I would just motion my hand toward Heaven for God to keep pouring it on, and each time I'd motion, another gully-washer of the Spirit would sweep over me. I didn't want this blessing to end, but suddenly it stopped, and the Holy Ghost revealed to me that I should go to a certain store in Bude, which was three miles away. I said, "God, I don't understand. I'm here in the Spirit, and You say go shopping. Okay, Lord, here I go!"

When I walked into the store, a lady came over to where I was and began a conversation. After a few words, I invited her to the revival, asking her if she had ever attended a Pentecostal church. "No, I never have," she answered, "but someone invited me to the revival last week. They didn't tell me that a lady was the evangelist. I believe I'll come."

Just that morning when I had gotten up, I had told Brother and Sister Murray, "I dreamed last night that the president came to our revival, and folks were gathered around speaking to him."

True to her promise, in walked the lady that night before service began. Church members gathered around her, welcoming her to the revival. Someone told me that she was the Chancery Clerk of Meadville. "There's my dream," I said to myself.

I was on my way home from the revival, just the Lord and I driving down the highway between Natchez and Little Rock, when I began to think of my mother. She had often said, "The Lord just gives you one step at a time. You take that step, and He will tell you what to do next."

I began talking to the Lord, telling Him, "I know I have been in Your perfect will in this revival. I wonder where You will lead me now."

Suddenly an angel of the Lord began singing in an audible voice: "I'm following Jesus one step at a time. Living in His presence that's so divine. Why think of tomorrow? Just live for today. I'm following Jesus each step of the way." At the end of the song each time, the last note would be held until I'd think that the singing had ended, but then he'd repeat the song.

After the singing had continued for a few miles, I said, "Lord, I know that this is an angel of the Lord." As I continued talking to the Lord, another voice joined in, singing tenor. They sang together for a few more miles, and then stopped suddenly, leaving quietness. I could hardly wait to share this experience with Brother Joel, my son, who is pastor of the home church. My heart burned within as I thought, "I've got to tell what happened today."

Please don't think that these experiences make me feel more righteous than other saints. That is not true at all. Doesn't the Bible say that angels are ministering spirits to the saints of God? The Lord just had them minister to me that day in a song. I was so thrilled, so thankful, and I wondered if it would ever happen again.

I continued working for the Lord, and I suppose it was a year later, August, 1987, when I flew to Brother and Sister Goff's in Kansas City for a revival. God blessed with a wonderful revival, filling souls with the Holy Ghost. I had purchased a one-way airline ticket since I hadn't known how long the revival would last. When it was time for me to return home, I started to call the airline, but Sister Goff said, "I'll call one of the ladies in the church and she'll make your reservation."

"Tell her to get me the cheapest fare," I told her. She purchased the ticket that evening. At the airport, bidding Sister Goff good-bye, I walked through the door to board the plane and found, to my surprise, steps going *down*, rather than up a ramp. I thought to myself, "What in this world am I in for?" Before me was a tiny prop plane which carried about twelve passengers. I was seated and awaiting takeoff when a lady came from inside the airport and said, "We have too many passengers. Would three of you like to volunteer to get off the plane?"

The Holy Ghost moved on me to volunteer. "Will they promise me another flight to Little Rock?" I asked.

"No," she answered. But I still felt led to get off the plane. I was afraid that Sister Goff may have already left, but when I walked back into the airport, her smiling face welcomed me.

I walked over to the ticket agent to check on a flight to Little Rock. "You will be flying on Delta, and we are giving you a check for $50.00 in appreciation for your volunteering to give up your seat on the other plane," she told me as she handed me a first-class ticket. I thought, "Lord, you are so kind."

"Lord, why are you doing all this?" I questioned. God always has a reason for what He does. We had a good flight during which I began to feel the presence of the Lord so near. In audible voices I heard angels singing. It sounded like a choir. They were singing, "I've been redeemed by love divine. Oh, glory, glory, He is mine! All to Him I now resign. I have been, I have been redeemed." They held the last note a long time just as the two angels had who had sung in the car.

It was wonderful to understand why the Lord had put me up there, away from the crowd. The angelic choir continued singing for about ten minutes. About fifteen minutes before we reached Memphis, they ceased. Then suddenly the intercom came on, and the pilot announced that we would be unable to land for about twenty-five minutes because of a severe storm directly over the airport. As we circled the airport I felt a touch of Heaven in my soul. I rejoiced, "Lord, land or fall, I've been redeemed!" This was August 7, 1987.

Chapter 23

Encamped by Angels

Once again, I was coming home from a revival in Brookhaven, Mississippi. Approaching Crystal Springs, I was undecided whether to stay on the freeway through Jackson or take a short cut, when an angel choir began to sing in audible voices. I said, "Lord, I'm not afraid to travel the narrow, crooked road." For forty miles I heard this choir.

Another experience I recall occurred the last week of December in 1989. Around four o'clock in the morning I awoke and did not feel sleepy at all. After lying awake for a few minutes, I got up and prayed. Although I wasn't sleepy, I lay back down and turned the light off. In the darkness of the room, I saw smoke over my bed as white as could be and an angel as bright as the light appeared with his wings stretched out. In just a few seconds, it all vanished away.

Lying there, many thoughts came to my mind. If I could only tell young people in this world how bright and beautiful one angel is! And to think that Heaven will have an innumerable company of those bright angels. Heaven is going to be so bright, but for those who miss Heaven, Hell will be so dark. Any sacrifice we need to make to please God will be worth it all.

In the spring of 1991, I was driving alone to Columbia, Mississippi, to preach a revival for Brother and Sister Terrell. Outside of Jackson, Mississippi, stopping to buy gas, I drove between the station and the gas pumps not far from the door. Mine was the only car at the station at this time. After filling the gas tank, I went in to pay. The attendant asked me what had happened to the person who was in the car with me when I drove into the station.

I said, "I'm traveling by myself." Then I thought, "I must talk to this man about his soul." It was another witness that there is always a purpose.

The last visitation I had of angels was March 9, 1992. The Spirit of the Lord led me to Tulsa, Oklahoma, for a revival in Brother and Sister Yeats's church. Traveling home alone from a revival a few miles out of Fort Smith, Arkansas, I began to hear a choir of audible voices singing an old song we used to sing many years ago, "Walking the Sea." They were such beautiful voices; I wish I could find words to describe them. As I listened to the words, "Walking the Sea," I thought, "I wonder, Lord, why You are doing this today." I'd noticed God always had a purpose. For a few miles I enjoyed this beautiful heavenly choir; then suddenly they stopped. A few miles farther, I began to face heavy, heavy rain, and it was hard to see the freeway; however, there was such a peace of God filling the car I couldn't have felt any safer if the sun had been shining brightly. I knew that when I could hardly see anything but water before me, there were other hands besides mine on the steering wheel.

All the way through the rain the Spirit of the Lord kept making Scriptures come alive in my soul about how the angels of the Lord encamp around about them that fear the Lord. I was so impressed with the part, that if we have His angels to encamp about us we must fear the Lord. If we fear the Lord, we will not pout or have an envious spirit against anyone. We will not have jealousy in our heart because the Bible says it's crueler than the grave. We will be afraid to speak unkind words because the Bible says charity suffers long and is kind. When we fear God, we rejoice with them that rejoice and weep with them that weep. When we fear God, we want to be very careful because it's " . . . the little foxes, that spoil the vines; for our vines have tender grapes" (Song of Solomon 3:15).

"Your glorying is not good. Know ye not that a little leaven leaveneth the whole lump? Purge out therefore the old leaven that ye may be a new lump, as ye are unleavened. For even Christ our Passover is sacrificed for us! Therefore let us keep the feast, not with old leaven, neither with the leaven of malice and wickedness; but with the unleavened bread of sincerity and truth" (Corinthians 5:6-8).

Moses commanded the children of Israel concerning the Passover, "Seven days shall you eat unleavened bread; even the first day ye shall put away leaven out of your houses: for whosoever eateth leavened bread from the first day until the seventh day, that soul shall be cut off from Israel" (Exodus 12:15).

We are told that before the Passover on the fourteenth day of the month the people searched with lighted candles even the darkest places in their houses to see if any leavened bread remained. Paul said, "For even Christ, our Passover is sacrificed for us" (I Corinthians 5:7). A perpetual sacrifice for us, therefore we, as the children of God, must put from us the leaven of evil. The whole life of a Christian should be a joyous and pure feast of serving God in sincerity and in truth. "Whereby, are given unto us exceeding great and precious promises: that, by these ye might be partakers of the divine nature, having escaped the corruption that is in the world through lust" (II Peter 1:4).

Living in an angel camp is one of these promises to a child of God. If we keep our part of the deal, God will never fail to keep His part. God is faithful. The Bible says, "He daily loadeth us with His benefits." That is talking about a big package of promises. When you choose to live for God, you are a blessed and privileged person.

People in this world are always seeking for help somewhere. Many resort to fortunetellers, to people with satanic power, as Saul did. Failing to keep the commandments of the Lord, when trouble came, he walked down a dark road seeking help from a witch who lived at Endor. When Saul lost the fear of the Lord from his heart, God's angels no longer encamped around him.

When Hagar fled from the house of Sarah, an angel of the Lord found her by a fountain of water in the wilderness. He knew who she was and from whence she had come. He told her to return to Sarah and submit herself under her hands. The angel knew she was expecting a child. He told her she would bear a son whose name would be Ishmael, and he would be blessed (Genesis 16:7-12). Angels know all things that are in the earth.

> To fetch about this form of speech hath thy servant Joab done this thing: and my Lord is wise, according to the wisdom of an angel of God, to know all things that are in the earth (II Samuel 14:20).

> Are they (angels) not all ministering spirits, sent forth to minister for them who shall be heirs of salvation (Hebrews 1:14)?

David wrote, "Bless the Lord, ye his angels, that excel in strength, that do his commandments, hearkening unto the voice of his word" (Psalm 103:20).

When the disciples came to Jesus asking, "Who is the greatest in the kingdom of Heaven," Jesus called a little child unto Him and set him down in the midst of them giving them a lesson in humility. "Take heed that ye despise not one of these little ones; for I say unto you, That in heaven their angels do always behold the face of my Father which is in heaven" (Matthew 18:10). Their angels are always looking into the face of God, ready to come to earth any second to minister any need of one of God's little ones. It is not only a child but also anyone who has been converted and has become as humble as a little child.

Two angels came with the Lord to the tent of Abraham and Sarah and ate lunch with Abraham. They had some good news for them; they were going to be blessed with a baby boy. But they also had sad news: the approaching destruction of Sodom and Gomorrah. As Abraham travailed before the Lord for the life of Lot and his family, the two angels went down to Sodom. There they found Lot sitting in the gate. He invited them into his house and made a feast. The Bible said they did eat. They spent the night with Lot and helped him, his wife, and two daughters hurry out of the city before it was destroyed. The angels literally took each of them by the hand and pulled them.

When Daniel was cast into the den of lions, the King rose early the next morning and running to the den of lions, he cried with a lamentable voice, "O Daniel, is thy God able to deliver thee from the lions?"

Daniel answered, "O King, my God hath sent his angel and has shut the lions' mouths, that they have not hurt me" (Daniel 6:20-22).

God sent an angel and walked Shadrach, Meshach, and Abednego around in the burning fiery furnace. Their clothes had no smell of fire (Daniel 3:27).

Esau hated his brother Jacob because their father had blessed Jacob. Esau said, "The days of mourning for my father are at hand. When my father is gone, I'm going to kill my brother."

These words were told to Rebekah, their mother. She called Jacob and said, "Your brother Esau has purposed in his heart to slay you. You must leave and stay away a few days until your brother's anger turns away."

She sent him to her brother who lived in Haran. What a sad day this must have been for Rebekah, Isaac, and Jacob as she packed Jacob's clothes. He told Dad and Mom goodbye and began his walk on a lonely road.

When the evening shadows began to fall and the sunset began to appear, Jacob decided he would camp for the night. Gathering some stones and piling them together for his pillow, he lay down to sleep. In a dream, he beheld a ladder set up on the earth with the top of it reaching to Heaven (God really has some long ladders). He saw angels of God ascending and descending; some coming down to earth while others, having fulfilled their mission, were returning to Heaven.

The wonderful part was that the Lord stood above the ladder. Then the Lord began to tell him how he was going to be blessed; even the land where he was lying would be given to him and to his seed. When he awoke, he said, "Surely the Lord is in this place, and I knew it not." No doubt, Jacob had felt so alone when he lay down and closed his eyes that evening, but he wasn't alone. He was lying near the gate of Heaven.

I imagine Jacob awakened the next morning feeling refreshed, the sun shining, the birds singing. That homesick feeling was gone because Jacob knew he was in God's perfect will with angels around and about him.

89

When he reached Haran, the first lady his eyes fell upon was Rachel, the one he would love and someday make his wife. God blessed everything Jacob touched during his stay of twenty years. And then the Lord spoke to Jacob to return to his homeland.

As Jacob obeyed, going on his way with his wives, sons, and his cattle, the angels of God met him. When Jacob saw them, he said, "This is God's host!" God has so many angels at His command that He can send a host of them to one of His children.

Jacob sent messengers before him to his brother Esau. When the messengers returned to tell him that Esau was on the way to meet him with four hundred men, Jacob was sore afraid. He feared that Esau was coming with an army to destroy him and his family. In his distress he called on the Lord for deliverance.

That night he was left alone and there wrestled with an angel. When the angel said, "Let me go, for the day breaketh," Jacob replied, " I will not let thee go, except thou bless me."

Jacob prevailed and received a new name, "Israel," which means "prince or power with God." Jacob called the name of that place "Penial," which means "the face of God."

This mighty experience was not the end of the story. Esau soon appeared, and he had four hundred men with him; but rather than approaching Jacob as an enemy, Esau ran to meet him, embraced him, fell on his neck and kissed him, even weeping.

Thank God for an innumerable company of angels.

Chapter 24

There Is a God in Heaven That Revealeth Secrets

Daniel 2:28

In 1965, Brother Holmes and the brethren erected a tabernacle on the campus of the Lakeview Children's Home, located on the Old Memphis Highway, where an old-fashioned camp meeting was conducted. Our hearts were thrilled as people gathered from many states to join with us in this camp meeting.

It was during this meeting that one Sunday evening before the regular service, I knelt in prayer (I still remember the very spot) and as the Spirit of the Lord came mightily upon me, I began to speak in other tongues. The Lord spoke the word "McConnell" and the face of my oldest son Ruebel came before me. I wondered what this could mean. When I got home from church that night, I mentioned the experience to Brother Holmes.

Occasionally I'd be praying and the Spirit of the Lord would make intercession; I would speak this word *McConnell*. I talked to different people, wondering if it could be some place the Lord was trying to reveal. I sought the Lord many times concerning this. The thought would go through my mind, "Could this be somebody or perhaps someplace overseas?"

About three years passed after the Lord had spoken; then some more words came. "I see a call, and it's a need. Just call them and see." Sometimes I would be awakened at three o'clock in the morning. These words would come so fluently that I would weep and ask the Lord to give me understanding.

One night I called my daughter Faith into the living room. I said, "Pray with me. Maybe this is concerning you." But then the Lord spoke through tongues and interpretation saying, "Have not I spoken to thee before?" I knew then that it did not concern a call in her life. What could this all mean? The question remained.

In the early part of 1970, I dreamed the auditorium of our church was ankle deep in water. I mentioned this to the church and said, "Do you suppose this means a revival?" But it was far from meaning a revival. Later, while the church was burning, the firemen filled it ankle deep with water.

In July we had a revival scheduled with Brother and Sister Springer in Biloxi, Mississippi. About a week before we left, I had another dream. I saw a number of the folks from the church, and we were lying down on the floor. I raised up and looked to see Brother Charles Dyson lying on the floor, too. I was impressed about this when I awoke.

While my two daughters and I were away in this revival, we had a telephone call from home. "The church is burning! It's burning to the ground!"

When the revival was over, we came home, driving first by the church, as usual. For the past twenty-five years if we were out somewhere, regardless of how late at night, Brother Holmes would always say, "Drive by the church." This time it was a pitiful sight to see. Only portions of burned walls were standing. But how good it was to be home and to see Brother Holmes and Brother Joel encouraged, keeping the banners waving for Jesus.

Brother Holmes said, "Who do you suppose called me early the next morning after the church burned? It was Brother Charles Dyson, who told me, 'I can help you. I have a friend who is a friend to your adjuster.'" Doesn't this remind you of the Scripture: "For the eyes of the Lord run to and fro throughout the whole earth to show himself strong in the behalf of them whose heart is perfect toward Him" (II Chronicles 16:9).

The next morning was Sunday and ten o'clock found the saints gathered under the old tabernacle for Sunday school. Until now I had been able to hold back the tears, but when I looked at those precious saints of God that Sunday morning under that old dilapidated tabernacle, I tried, but in vain. The tears poured. It had been five years since we had met there. Everybody seemed encouraged. This was the third service since the church had burned. Different ones kept contending that everything would be all right.

I began awakening early in the morning. The Spirit would speak, "Just call them and see." One morning about three o'clock, I was in the living room, and began feeling victory concerning this. I started leaping and shouting. The Lord impressed me that it wouldn't be long until I would know what this all meant. I told Brother Joel the next morning that there was someone the Lord wanted us to call, and I believed that it was concerning this new church. He said, "Mama, just start calling." I didn't know whom to call.

It was about four days until time for the annual camp meeting. Faith and Brother Joel were busy at the Children's Home making preparations for the meeting. I had just finished preparing supper when Ruebel, our oldest son, walked in. After supper we went for a drive in the north part of town on McCain Boulevard, where there were several acres of vacant land. It looked beautiful; Brother Holmes and I were impressed. We thought that this would make a good location for the new church. As we talked on our way back, I asked if they thought the owner of the property would sell. Ruebel said, "Just call him and see."

It seemed like those words almost jarred the car. I said, "Well, I've been saying that for a long time." Brother Holmes agreed. That very evening we called. The answer was yes, and it would cost $8,000 an acre.

That night we prayed and fleeced the Lord that if this were the place that the Lord wanted us to have, the businessman's heart would be touched to give us a better price. The next morning he called and told us

Sis. Holmes

93

that since it would be for a church, he would take $6,000 an acre. This man's name was none other than McConnell! He was the same man who was the friend to the adjuster Brother Dyson had called about. Isn't the Lord wonderful! This was one of the most inspiring experiences in my Christian walk.

The last confirmation was another dream. In this dream, Brother Holmes and one of the brethren, Brother Haney, were standing out in the street in front of this land. The Lord appeared and started singing a chorus of a song. These were the words: "If Jesus said it, I believe it. His word cannot lie. If it's written in the Bible, I'll believe it 'till I die. Though the mountains be removed and cast into the sea, The word of God will stand throughout eternity."

I awoke, and throughout the rest of the night, this voice would awake me saying, "Jesus said it. His word cannot lie." This was a wonderful night. The next day I felt the presence of the Lord so close. I promised the Lord that I would never doubt this. At the time we were moving into a building program for a new church. Mr. McConnell, about whom the Lord had spoken to me five years before (I didn't know him, and had never heard of him.), was a contractor. He was the builder of the new church at Fifty-second Place.

Chapter 25

The Mission Fields

It was early in the sixties when we became acquainted with Brother and Sister Williams from Tulsa, Oklahoma. Our lives were enriched by the fellowship of these dedicated folks. They had great convictions and such a burden for the work of God.

Attending each other's camp meetings and conventions, we had many wonderful times together. They have gone on to be with the Lord now. I'm thankful that their granddaughter, Sister Jan Williams Yeats, who is married to Brother Michael Yeats, has picked up the torch and is carrying it on.

One of Sister Williams's favorite Scriptures was: ". . . Eat the fat, and drink the sweet, and send portions unto them for whom nothing is prepared." They desired so much that Brother Holmes and I would also get the burden for mission work and invited us to go with them to Mexico and South America to visit some of their works. With the church, old folks' home, and Christian school, Brother Holmes felt that he pretty well had his hands full.

Sister Marilyn Smith (Sister Harold Tetrick) went with me to the Williams's church for a revival. When the revival closed, Brother and Sister Williams, Sister Marilyn and I met Brother Holmes in Indiana at a conference. The first night Sister Williams talked about Brother Morar's work in India, of how he was pastoring three churches and had never owned a car. As she was talking, the Holy Ghost moved on me to stand up when she sat down to say that I would give the amount which I had in my purse, which was $97.00, that I had been given in the revival at Tulsa. Well, I thought about not being able to ask Brother Holmes, so I sat there and failed God. When we got to the motel room, I told Brother Holmes about the experience, and he said, "You know I wouldn't have cared."

First trip to Brazil
Sis. Holmes with Rev. and Mrs. J. N. Holmes

Sis. Holmes and Sis. Jan

First trip to Brazil; Rev. & Mrs. J. N. Holmes, Sis. Holmes, Rev. & Mrs. Raul Alvear

Second trip to Brazil; (L to R) Sis. Judie Weaver, Sis. Edna Lucas, Sis. Angie Looper, Sis. Holmes,
Sharon Brewer, Andrea & Renee, Faith Cavin, Justin Brewer, Nicole Cavin, Nathan Holmes,
Chelsea Cavin, Sis. Janet Holmes

Sis. Alvear and Sis. Holmes preaching in San Paulo

Missionary from Brazil: Brad Lambeth, Nara Lambeth, and Ana Paula Lambeth

*Sis. Holmes, Sis. Alvear, Sis. George
Second trip to Brazil outside Valinhos Church*

Sis. Alvear and Sis. Holmes in Brazil

97

Then I felt so bad and could never forgive myself because I thought, "No doubt, if I had obeyed, others would have been moved to give, and the brother could have had a car." This was the first time I remember hearing about the Morars.

Fifteen years passed and one camp meeting when Brother Morar was in the States, he came to our camp meeting and stayed in our home. One night when he was talking about his work in India, I asked him, "Brother Morar, do you have a car?" "No, Sister Holmes," he replied, "I've never owned a car." I said, "Brother Morar, I'll give the first hundred dollars on a car for you." Then Brother Joel spoke up and said, "And I'll give the second." I was so thrilled that after fifteen years, God had given me another chance to obey Him. Brother Joel took him to other churches and when he returned to India, he had money to buy a new van.

In 1983, Brother Joel and Sister Jan decided to make a trip to visit the Alvears and the Lambeths in Brazil and invited me to go with them. I've never liked to fly, always preferring to go by car. However, my great desire to take this trip made me willing to fly. About three days before we were leaving, while lying in bed early one morning I said, "Lord, you know I'm afraid to fly. You are going to have to help me." All at once it was like something flashed on a screen at the foot of my bed; it was Sister Alvear with a big smile on her face. I said, "Thank you, Lord, I know I'm going to make it to Brazil even if I don't make it back."

We were sitting in the airport in Little Rock when we were told that the plane would be delayed because the fog was too bad to land in St. Louis. After about an hour, we left for St. Louis, although the fog was still heavy. When the plane turned its direction, we weren't very high, but it seemed as if we could just be spilled out! I had a homesick feeling and said, "Oh, Lord, why did I get on this plane?" All went well, however, and we landed safely in St. Louis.

When we left St. Louis for Miami, it was still foggy. I thought, "I'll be glad when we get to the sunshine state of Florida." Well, soon the sun was shining beautifully through the windows of the aircraft, and I felt happy to be flying. I told Brother Joel and Sister Jan, "This is much better than being home washing dishes."

The first time the speaker came on, the pilot announced how high we were flying and informed us that in fifteen minutes we would be flying over Tallahassee, Florida. Well, we never heard any more about Tallahassee. When the speaker came on the next time, we were told, "Buckle your safety belts; we are entering a pretty bad storm. It's so low we can't get under it and we are flying as high as we can fly. It reaches so wide, we can't go around, so we are going to have to go through it." Then the sunshine was gone, and it was more like we were riding a horse than flying. I said, "Sister Jan, I appreciate that vision I had of Sister Alvear." She said, "I do, too."

I learned little lessons from this. One is that there are storms in life that you cannot go around; you just have to buckle your safety belt and go through them. Another is to be happy where you are. I was down in St. Louis because of fog, and longing for the sunshine of Florida. My sunshine turned out to be a storm. Then I thought, "St. Louis wasn't so bad after all." We were over an hour late getting to Miami.

The next day about noon we walked through customs in Sao Paulo and I saw my vision for real: the smiling faces of Brother and Sister Alvear meeting us. We were in for a wonderful time with service that night and each night thereafter. We met some of the sweetest saints. After spending about a week there, the Alvears drove us to Rio de Janeiro. After a couple of days of sightseeing, we flew from there to visit with the Lambeths.

The morning before we left the Alvears' home, a pastor's wife, Sister Jose, came over to tell us good-bye. Brother Jose had caught the bus to go to Bahia in northern Brazil. A few weeks before I left the States, the Holy Ghost spoke over and over, "Go to Bahiki!" I asked Sister Taylor, Sister Alvear's mother, if she remembered a place in Brazil by that name, but she said that she didn't. I talked also to Sister Alvear about this name, but she couldn't think of the place either.

We flew to the Lambeth's work about a thousand miles from Rio. It was another happy day when we saw the smiling faces of the Lambeth family. You can't imagine how much you appreciate smiles until you are in a far country and don't know many folks. I think of missionaries who have stepped on foreign soil with no one that they knew to meet them. Bless their hearts; their rewards will be great on the other side.

We had the time of our life visiting with Brother and Sister Lambeth, their family, and some of their works in Brazil. They took us to the mountains sightseeing, and we met some of the finest saints, whose faces we will never forget. After two weeks we got back to the good old state of Arkansas.

One day after I had returned home from Brazil, Sister Taylor (Sister Alvear's mother) said, "I had a letter from Sister Alvear and she said to tell you the word the Holy Ghost was speaking to you, "Bahiki" in English would be "Bahia" in Portuguese." I thought, "Well, no doubt the Lord was just confirming Brother Jose's going up there to work for God."

A few months later, I had a letter from the Lambeths inviting me to come back and preach in some of their churches. Brother Lambeth wrote in the letter, "We want you to stay at least two weeks here, and I know you will want to visit the Alvears. Some of us will accompany you there so you won't have to travel alone."

Service at Home Church

Some of my friends in Brazil

Brother Jose's house and church in Cacule

100

Second trip to Brazil; (L to R) Kristen & David Beall, Sis. Juanita Beall, Sis. Jan Holmes, Rev. J. N. Holms, Chuck Cavin (background), Sis. Holmes, Faith Cavin, Sis. Sarah Isbell holding Jennifer, Bro. Isbell, Sis. Cherree Looper holding grandson Dustin, Bro. Danny Looper, Joey Brewer, Renee Brewer, Nathan Holmes, Chelsea & Nicole Cavin

Justin was very sad
at my leaving for Brazil

Sis. Holmes, Bro. Terry Isbell, and Rev. & Sis. Raul Alvear

Bro. Danny Looper and Bro. Raul Alvear

101

The Holy Ghost would ever so often speak "Bahiki."

One night I had a dream that I was meeting my mother, who had gone to be with the Lord several years before. In the dream one of my aunts, Julia Hutto, who is also deceased, was with her and they were both smiling. When I tried to embrace them, they both withdrew from me as if they did not want me to touch them. Then I looked to see a mixed crowd of people, some dark and some white. I began to preach to them about the plan of salvation. I awoke feeling so impressed. I told Brother Joel about the dream and his interpretation was, "Mother, it sounds like you have some more work to do for the Lord."

A few days after this dream, I was in the Spirit when the Lord took hold of my tongue and spoke in English, "Go to Bahia first." I thought, "I don't know how this can work out. Brother Lambeth said to come there and then they would help me get to the Alvears, but whatever, Lord." The Spirit began to speak, "Go by sea," and to say through me, "I'm sailing." I felt in the Holy Ghost that God was leading me back to Brazil.

Little did I know then that within a few days my telephone would ring and I would hear Sister C. E. George saying, "I'm leaving the first day of January for the Alvears. My son was going but due to changing jobs, he can't get away. Sister Alvear called and said for me to get in touch with you, that you might come with me."

I asked, "Are you going to Bahia?"

"Yes, we will arrive at the Alvears Saturday and leave Monday for Bahia," she answered.

Sis. Veta, Brother Arnold Dedmon and Sis. Holmes

I said, "Yes, I'll go." There would have been no way I could have gotten a visa that soon but I was able to take her son's place, and everything could be arranged in time to leave.

We were met by Brother and Sister Alvear in Sao Paulo, then went on to Campinas, where they live. We were in service that night and the next day. Monday night we were in service at one of their churches across town. After service, twelve of us left in a little mini van for Bahia. Since Brother and Sister Alvear had been in the States, they had promised their children this trip. The small van was about ten years old and the bottom had rusted out and had been repaired. There's no telling how many motors had been rebuilt for it. I thought, "These missionaries need a new van so bad." We had the biggest mountains to travel over; it seemed we would almost fly down the mountain so we could make it up the next one.

On one stop along the way, we had a great service in which two received the Holy Ghost. We ate supper with this pastor; then about ten or eleven that night we started out for Bahia. Sister Alvear had gone to the grocery store and bought food for lunch the next day. I really couldn't tell what she was getting because I couldn't read the language on the cans. About ten o'clock the next day we stopped and had a picnic lunch. They broke open that bread, a little hard roll, and put sardines in it. The tails of those fish were sticking out. Suddenly I did not feel hungry at all. I decided to put myself on a fast right then and there.

I kept thinking all day, "When are we getting to Bahia?" I never dreamed it was thirteen hundred miles from where we had started Monday

Traveling wib the Alvears in Brazil

night. Brother Alvear had sent the pastor, Brother Jose, a telegram to meet us around 3:00 p.m. Wednesday at the city park in this little town. Such mountains that we traveled over I had never seen before in my entire life. About eight o'clock Tuesday night Sister Alvear said, "Sister Holmes, you have got to be hungry." I was riding along thinking about what the hobo said during the Depression. Late in the evening as he was walking through the country, he approached a house, knocked on the door, and said "Lady, I'm so hungry, and I don't know where I'm going to sleep tonight."

Sister Alvear said, "I don't know what you will eat, but I know where you will sleep: in this van!" Well, that's where I had slept sitting up the night before, but I was feeling fine.

About the time we stopped laughing, someone said, "Look! That looks like a good place to eat." It was delicious food. We had a feast and resumed our journey into the night.

Around 3:30 Wednesday afternoon we arrived at the city park. I looked up and here came Brother Jose, a little cap on his head and a big smile on his face. We found a hotel in which to stay, quite different from the ones back home; the shower and bathrooms were outside. Don't get me wrong; there are nice hotels in many places in Brazil, even nicer than the hotels here. However, this place to which we had traveled was very crude; stores had no refrigeration. We had to rush around and all get a shower and dress for church.

Then taking Brother Jose in the van with us, we began our trip twenty miles to where he had service announced for us that night. For a few

Brother Jose wading water full of snakes in the Interior

104

miles we traveled on a paved road; then we turned onto a very rough and narrow road. I knew nothing about back in the interior, but I was about to get my first lesson. Finally we came to where the road was covered with water. Brother Alvear said, "That looks too deep," and stopped the van. Brother Jose pulled off his shoes and waded across, seeking help to get us all across. While we were sitting waiting, Sister Alvear and Sister George were begging to get out and wade across. About that time a man walked up to the van and Brother Alvear asked if there were any snakes in the water. He said, "Yes, it's full of little poisonous snakes."

Sister Alvear and Sister George said, "We won't be afraid to wade across." I've always been afraid of snakes. I said, "I'm staying on this side of Jordan!"

The next thing we knew a man came with a cart pulled by a mule. Another man carried a little brass light. They told Sister George, Sister Alvear, and me to get into the cart. The wheels were very high, so it was all we could do to get in. Sister George had her camera and was snapping pictures when Sister Alvear interrupted her, "Don't flick the camera or the mule will run away!"

"He probably will anyway," I thought. We had a little hill to go down. When we got to the bottom, the mule couldn't pull us all; the load was too heavy. When the Brazilian man beat the mule with a stick, he tried; but he just couldn't move us. We were in the water, but Sister George and Sister Alvear jumped out. I was crying out, "Let me out!" but the little wagon was already moving. Neither the driver nor the one carrying the light could understand what I was saying. I was yelling, "Stop!" The mule didn't understand English either, so they carried me on across. There sat an old pickup truck. They helped me to get in where I could wait as they went back for others. Brother Alvear and the children decided to stay and not come across. They went to a house we had just passed and had a church service with some people there.

Soon we were going down a little crooked road; by this time it was about 9:00 p.m. At the end of the road sat a little house in which the man who owned the truck lived. Service, however, was in a house across a field. Brother Jose left us, running ahead to tell the folks not to give up on us, that we were on our way. A little boy was carrying a tiny brass lamp for us to walk by. We could hardly see and could see no light across the field where the service was. I said, "Sister Alvear, where is the house?"

She answered, "It's over there." Some kind of grass and burrs were scratching our legs; they said that we would have a small stream of water to cross yet. I stopped and lifted my hands as high toward heaven as I could reach and as loudly as I could, I hollered, "Help, God! Help, God!" I thought, "Lord, you have always come to my rescue." They were all

105

Having a house meeting in Brazil

laughing, but it had become serious with me. As we stood there a minute waiting for God to do something, we saw an old man, who appeared to be in his seventies, approaching us. He said, "Go back to the house." He was referring to the one in which the owner of the pickup truck lived. The old man continued, "The people are coming to you." We were only a few steps from that house. I said, "Thank you, Jesus! You are always there."

At 9:30 we were ready to begin service. Brother Jose said, "Missionary," speaking to Sister Alvear, "don't expect me to cut this service short! These people need to hear from God." We had a service and it was Thursday morning by the time we got back to the hotel. We hadn't seen a bed since Sunday night. We were receiving a little sample of a missionary's life. I know it was a miracle, but I did not feel too tired, although I was sixty-five years old at this time. They all laughed when I made the remark, "I'm glad the Lord didn't wait until I was old to call me to work in the mission field!"

We had service the next night in the little town where we were staying. Brother Jose's wife and children were at their home sixty miles away in another town. We left Friday going home with Brother Jose.

On the way the Holy Ghost dealt with me about a sermon Brother Joel had preached about crucifying the flesh. He illustrated as he preached, "Just catch the back of your neck and pull this old flesh down." I recalled how he grasped his own coat at the back of his neck and forced himself around, making a lasting impression. "Lord," I said, "I get the message; you want me to crucify the flesh." The Holy Ghost would keep saying, "Send a portion for whom nothing has been prepared." Over and over

I could hear those words.

We finally reached the home of Brother Jose, finding the smiling faces of his wife and children waiting to welcome us. On Saturday morning, I was standing outside the house when Brother Jose came walking from the market where he had bought a big beautiful beef roast. It was unwrapped; he was just holding it in his hands. The sellers had traveled all night bringing this meat to market in ox carts without refrigeration in over 100-degree weather. He was so thrilled that he could do this special thing for us.

We were in service Saturday night there in their church; then Sunday morning Brother Alvear hired a man with a pickup truck to take everyone eighteen miles back to one of Brother Jose's churches in the Interior. Normally, the Jose family would leave about five o'clock on Sunday morning and walk there. The back of the truck was packed full by the time we all got in. A sister, who came on the trip, and I were honored to ride in the front with the driver. The road was rough and the dust was flying, but soon he parked in front of this little church.

It rested on five acres of land. Brother Jose's grandfather had given him this small tract of land and he had donated it to build a church. It was the only land he had ever owned. One thing I noticed in those Brazilian saints was that they delighted in giving anything they owned to the Lord.

In front of the church I was surprised to see a cart about four by four with two big long-horned oxen harnessed to it. After service I learned that they were afraid I wouldn't be able to walk the next seven miles to the house where we would have the night service. The man with the truck

On the way to Interior in an ox cart. I was 65 years old and it was 7 miles to the next service. Some of the brethren thought I was too old to walk that far, I really wasn't. The temperature was 110°.

had gone back to town. When the morning service was over Sister Pauli and I were honored again. We crawled up on the little ox cart with tall wooden wheels, and the owner walked as he drove the oxen down a rough trail with big rocks.

I had noticed when we left the little town early that morning that they were carrying a carton with a dozen and a half eggs. I wondered why but thought, "I guess I'll learn the reason." The cart ride was so rough that some of the eggs broke as they rested in Sister Pauli's lap. The temperature was about 110 degrees, but the crowd walked behind the cart the seven miles in the mid-day heat. I thought, "I guess it pays off sometimes to be old." The farther along the road we went, the rougher it got. Finally, I decided I wanted to walk the rest of the way.

As we were walking, I asked Brother Alvear why the wife of the man who had brought the ox hadn't come. He said, "She stayed at home to work on the stove." I thought, "Well, I guess her stove was torn up." I hated to keep asking so many questions, but I was soon to learn the entire story. When we reached their home (a humble-looking place with a big muddy pond), we discovered that his wife had stayed home to cook lunch for us.

A little woman who had attended service that morning lived seven kilometers farther. As she started walking on home, I felt so sorry for her knowing she had already walked twenty-one kilometers that day. I asked Sister Alvear why she didn't stay and eat lunch with us. She replied, "She has to go home and cook for her husband, who is unsaved." I thought, "Now she will be walking back seven kilometers to the service here tonight; it looks like he could cook himself some rice and beans!" My mother used to get in sympathy with women folks sometimes saying, "There won't be enough men in Heaven to sing bass!"

This little lady who had stayed home to prepare our lunch had cooked the roast her husband had bought Saturday at the same market from where the other roast had come. They had no refrigeration in their home. She cooked spaghetti and I knew the water for the spaghetti had come from the muddy pond. These folks were so sweet and humble; they wouldn't dare eat a bite before they saw that we were filled. Three times I have gone to Brazil, and God has blessed me to never get sick from the food or water. After lunch they showed me a room where I could rest. There was a half bed with a straw mattress.

Early in the evening people began to gather for service. Little kerosene lanterns were strung up outside, and a couple of benches were placed in the yard. Here came the little lady who had walked on home to cook for her husband. About seventy-five people stood for service. After service it began raining and people began walking home without even a flashlight through trails in the dark woods. I thought of the faithful woman who had gone home to prepare lunch for her husband. She had walked forty-two miles that day to worship the Lord, and she didn't have a pew to sit on that night. I remembered the Scripture the Holy Ghost had spoken Friday as we rode along, "Give a portion to whom nothing has been prepared." I thought, "God, when you said nothing, you *meant* nothing." There had not been even a seat prepared for her.

I finally found out why the eggs had been carried so far that day, first in a pickup truck and then in the ox cart. Sister Alvear had boiled them that day, while the lady was finishing lunch, for the children to eat that night after church on their way back to Brother Jose's home. The owner of the pickup truck returned from town to pick us up. While we were riding back, the boiled eggs were passed around for a snack. We left for home the next morning. After traveling three or four days, we pulled up in front of the home of the Alvears just as the motor went out on the van.

Our next trip was by bus to Paraguay, which was about seven hundred miles away. Another new experience awaited me. Sister Alvear had mentioned several times, "When we go on this trip, we always enjoy getting to buy fried catfish on the river while we are waiting to cross the ferry." I pictured a beautiful river with snow-white sandbars and people cooking catfish in beautiful stainless steel cookers on neat stands. When we finally got there, I received the surprise of my life. Mud was ankle deep; there was no white sand, no stainless steel cookers. After my first look, I said to myself, "This looks like the dump."

I laughed, "I guess what the problem is, if I were going to be a good missionary, I should have started earlier in life." Sister George would

Sis. George and I at the market in Cacule where Brother Jose lives.

laugh when I'd say, "I'm glad I never waited until I was old to be a missionary." I'm sure sixty-five sounded old to Sister George!

Our next trip was to Paraguay Border Church about 250 miles from Campinas. Brother and Sister Alvear, Sister George, and I went by bus. Another new experience awaited me. There are no air-conditioners on the buses and since the Brazilian people believe that the tropical air will make you sick if it blows on you, if anyone opened the vent in the top of the bus, someone else would get up and close it. We traveled all night and most of the following day, reaching Paraguay Border Church in time for service that night.

I experienced a miracle in one of the churches about two hundred miles from Campinas. It was a Sunday evening service; since the crowded building was without fan or air-conditioning, the temperature inside was at least 120 degrees. Just after the service began, a little sister with tears rolling down her cheeks suddenly rose from her seat about the middle of the church and began dancing in the Spirit. Within an instant I, too, felt the Spirit of dance and began dancing. I danced for quite some time. The Lord put a cool wind around me, like an air conditioner. I was amazed beyond words. I'll never forget this experience as long as I live. That has been perhaps fifteen years ago, but every time I testify about this I feel the Spirit of the Lord!

We spent the whole month of January in Brazil. I wondered if the Holy Ghost would ever lead me again that far away from home.

About a couple of years passed. One night as I was standing in my laundry room praying, feeling the Spirit of the Lord so close, I began speaking in tongues. Then in English the Spirit spoke, "Go by sea! Go by sea! Go by sea!" Shocked, I said, "Lord are you telling me to go to Brother and Sister Springer's church at Biloxi? That's by the sea." Then like tongues of fire I spoke, "No! I'm sailing." I knew then that the Lord was sending me back to South America.

I fleeced the Lord for further witness. I asked the Lord that if he wanted me to go to South America to talk to Sister Alvear about it. In a week or two, I received a letter from her asking me to come and preach in some of their churches. I told the Lord, "I'm not going to answer this. I want you to deal with her some more." In a few weeks here came another letter saying, "Sister Holmes, the saints are asking for you to come." Then I answered that letter telling her how the Holy Ghost had talked to me.

I dreaded to go that far alone. I remembered Brother Danny Looper and Brother Terry Isbell had told me when I returned home the time before that if I ever went back, they wanted to go too. Both of them made the trip with me and spent a week there. It was a great blessing for them to accompany me. I bought my ticket to stay thirty days. We visited

Last trip to Brazil; Bro. Terry Isbell, Sis. Holmes and Bro. Danny Looper

The Alvears, Bro. Danny, Bro. Terry, friends in Brazil, and Sis. Holmes

Friends in Brazil

many churches and had some great services.

After I had been there about a week, the Lord moved on me to fast three days. While I was fasting, the Lord would wake me up during the night and talk to me about the life of a missionary and their "labor under pressure." They travel hundreds of miles to their works feeling the pressure of the possibility of family dying and not being able to attend the funeral. Since there is no embalming in that country, people are buried the day after their death. Every few months missionaries must leave their field of labor, fly back to the States and visit churches all over the country asking for support enabling them to stay on the mission field. Sometimes preachers are not even too thrilled to have them.

The Lord said, "This is not right. If people would obey Scripture, 'Send a portion to whom nothing has been prepared,' they wouldn't be under this pressure." One night as I lay in bed during the midnight hour, I thought of the many saints there who did not have sufficient food and had bad water to drink. The Lord said, "One day they will neither thirst any more nor hunger any more." At this time the Alvears' transportation was worn out. I just kept this all in my heart and pondered it.

The last trip we made was back to Paraguay Border Church during the first of November. Although it was cold, there was no heat in the house. My teeth were chattering as I looked at the cover on the little cot and saw the English print "U-Haul." I knew what had happened. Someone from the States had sent Sister Alvear a U-Haul cover and she had cut it into pieces, sharing it with this pastor's wife. It looked good on such a cold night with no heat in the house.

The next morning the Alvears, the pastor, and his wife were making preparations to go check on a saint who was ill. We had traveled by car seven hundred miles to this place. It felt so good lying on the cot that morning. I told Sister Alvear, "If it's all right, I believe I'll stay here today and pray for the service here tonight."

The pastor's son and his girlfriend decided to stay with me although I couldn't speak their language, and they could not understand me. About twelve o'clock I got hungry, and we went into the kitchen and attempted to communicate by motions. I had bought a sack of Irish potatoes for this family Saturday evening. They couldn't afford to buy potatoes and were so thrilled to get them. We ate French fries and smiled at each other. After a while I felt really hungry. I thought, "I have some money and if I could talk to them, I'd ask them to go with me to the store where I'd buy a watermelon, some bananas, and cookies. But there's no way I can communicate, so I'll have to wait. Maybe we'll have something to eat after church."

Just about sundown the folks returned from the trip. Sister Alvear,

This is the banana tree the pastor's wife took me to make this picture in their back yard.

who entered the house first, handed me a package of cookies and said, "Brother Alvear is bringing in a watermelon for you." I could hardly believe my eyes. Entering then, the pastor's wife went straight to the bedroom and returned with a camera in her hand. Sister Alvear said, "Sister Holmes, follow her; she wants to take your picture in front of the banana tree in the back yard." I thought to myself, "It's too dark. Why doesn't she wait until the morning?" She motioned for me to stand right there by the tree. I looked and it was a banana tree with ripe bananas. After snapping the picture, she motioned for me to pull a banana. I pulled one, then she made me understand to pull another one. I went into the house eating one ripe banana, and holding another one in my hand. I didn't know there were ripe bananas in the yard. About that time, her husband come bringing a knife and cut the whole bunch. I thought to myself, "Lord, you beat all I've ever seen! You left out nothing that I desired to eat."

The day came for me to board that big aircraft for my return home. Although I had been gone only a month, I was homesick to see my grandchildren and children. Just think of the sacrifice made by missionaries in staying away from their loved ones for such prolonged periods. The way I feel, the red carpet should be rolled out for them when they return home.

It seemed God walked with me every step of the way home! Since I have had some problems with my back, I knew my suitcases were too heavy for me to lift in going through customs. When it looked as if everyone in the plane were asleep sometime that morning, I knelt on my knees and the Holy Ghost started making intercession. I said, "Lord, I'm asking you to get my luggage from the conveyor." Soon we reached Miami. I was walking from the plane to claim my luggage when a woman that I hadn't noticed before on the plane asked me, "Are you traveling alone?"

I replied, "Yes."

"I'm going to lift your suitcase off for you," she said.

I said, "Oh, I'm afraid they will be too heavy for you."

"No, you should see how heavy mine are!" she exclaimed.

I thought, "Lord, here you are again. I didn't even have to ask anyone!"

I arrived at the airport in Little Rock about one o'clock Tuesday. After a short visit, Brother Joel said, "Mother, tomorrow night I want you to tell the church about your trip." I still felt the message on my heart that God had given me while I was fasting. I said to Brother Joel in the study Wednesday evening, "Brother Joel, when I share what God has given me, the church is going to be moved and I don't want you to feel I'm trying to go over your head."

Thank God for such a wonderful, God-fearing and God-loving son. He said, "Mother, you obey God. I want the will of the Lord."

My text was, "Laboring under Pressure." When I finished, I said, "I don't feel I have done a very good job getting up here and stammering around."

When Brother Joel came to the pulpit, he said, "Mother said she didn't think she had done a very good job, but I know it's been worth fifteen hundred dollars because while she was talking, someone sent me a fifteen hundred dollar check for Brazil." He continued, "I'm going to place the drum out here before the pulpit and let everyone obey the Lord." Nine thousand dollars was given to help buy the Alvears a van. With tear-filled eyes, I looked up to Heaven and said, "Lord, I know now why you said, 'Go back to Brazil'."

Returning home from Brazil

114

Chapter 26

✝

Guy, Arkansas

One day as I was praying and seeking the Lord, I began speaking in tongues and the Spirit spoke these words through me in English: "Go to Guy." Brother George Guy, my cousin, was pastoring a church in Vidalia, Louisiana. I said, "Lord, if you are wanting me to go there for a revival, deal with him to call me." I thought, "It's so strange, Lord, that you would call him Guy."

Many weeks passed, during which time when the Spirit would be making intercession, I would speak, "Go to Guy." I'd say, "Lord, Brother Guy has never called me." One day when I was praying and spoke these words, the Holy Ghost revealed, "It's Guy, Arkansas."

I thought, "Lord, looks like I would have thought of this when you first spoke because Guy is only fifty miles away!"

Brother and Sister Burr, the parents of Sister Jan Holmes, lived in Texas but had bought a farm about five miles from Guy. Brother Joel called me within the next few days after the Lord had revealed that it was Guy, Arkansas. He said, "Mother, we are going up to Brother Burr's place to spend the night. Do you want to go with us?" I hadn't mentioned to him about my feeling a burden for that area. I said, "Yes. The Lord is dealing with me about that area."

The next morning I awoke and began praying, "Lord, what do you want?" Just as plain as day, the Spirit revealed these words: "It's a fountain sealed. It's a well shut up." I could hardly wait to tell Brother Joel and Sister Jan what the Lord had just spoken.

When I told them, Brother Joel said, "Let's ride around and see who we can find." The first place we stopped was by a trailer with a garden growing near it. It belonged to Brother Gene Rowlett and his wife, who lived in California. Still owning land in Guy where they were from, they often came and spent a few months there in the summer.

Brother Joel said, "Brother Rowlett, Mother feels a burden for Guy." Brother Rowlett said, "Let me tell you what someone told me. Many years ago when holiness was first preached in Arkansas, a Pentecostal minister came here in a horse and buggy and began a meeting, but the people rejected him so viciously that they cut off his horse's tail! He closed the meeting and left town."

To my ears, this was just like Gideon in the Bible, who went down behind the tents and heard the dream and the interpretation. I said, "Yes, that's my fountain the Lord talked to me about this morning."

Soon I gathered up some gospel tracts and went back to Guy, which has a population of less than two hundred. The very first door I knocked on, a lady, a member of the Beard family, invited me in. As I began telling her about my burden, she started wiping tears. I told her I wanted to find a place in which to have some services. She said, "Let me tell you what a friend of mine, who goes to the Baptist church, said the other day. She said, 'I wish some Pentecostal folks would come here and build a church'." Again, I felt like Gideon down by the tents. Sister Beard continued, "I have some friends that live a couple of miles from here. Would you go and tell them what you have told me?"

I drove over to the Woods family and told them about my desire. They were excited and said, "If you can find a place, we will sure come."

We searched for some empty building, but there seemed to be no place to hold services. I even made another trip back to look.

Brother Joel met a man who was working on his lawn mower, and he mentioned to him about my feeling a burden to preach in Guy. One day this man called Brother Joel long distance and said, "I've found your mother a place to preach." He said it's twenty-something miles from here at Naylor, Arkansas, in a community church. The man in charge said, "Tell her to come."

Well, I went to Naylor where there was no pastor. The people were Baptist and Assembly of God. I went two or three weekends and really enjoyed being with them, but I thought, "This is not Guy. The Holy Ghost said, 'Go to Guy.'"

Years passed, but I could not shake the burden. Everywhere I went to preach a revival I'd always tell the pastor that I felt a burden for Guy, Arkansas. Even in Brazil, I talked about it to the Alvears and Sister Lambeth. I remember Sister Lambeth said, "Sister Holmes, when you get back to the States, if you don't see but one soul saved at Guy, it will be worth everything." I purposed in my heart that I would go.

Years passed, and then one day, I thought, "How can I face God when I haven't obeyed Him about going to Guy? Could it be I've waited too long?" I was scared. I lifted my hands and prayed. "Lord, if you still want me to go to Guy, give me one more witness, and I'll never doubt."

A couple of days after praying this prayer, I stopped at a service station about three miles from my home since my car's gas gauge was on empty. I filled the tank and walked in to pay for the gas. When I handed the cashier my credit card, she said, "Did you know that your card is expired?" I said no that I didn't know it. A young woman, who was standing behind me, handed the cashier her card and said, "Put that on my card." Since she was a total stranger, I said no telling the cashier not to accept it, but this lady insisted. I said to the woman, "This embarrasses me. Do you realize that's almost thirty dollars worth of gas?"

She said, "Well, if you feel badly for me to do it, I'll give you my name and address, and if you want to send me a check sometime it will be all right." I told her I sure would and thanked her. When I got to the car, I looked at this paper to find that she was from a small town near Guy.

I said, "God, I'll never doubt that you want a church at Guy." In a few days I wrote her a few lines thanking her for her kindness and telling her about my burden for Guy. I thought that maybe something would open up for services through her so I mailed the letter with a check. It went to the post office address she had given me, and then to another small town nearby. Then the letter came back saying that she had moved and left no address.

Not very long after this, a young evangelist from our church, Brother Mike Blakley, who had been evangelizing with his wife and son, came home for a visit. He called me and said, "Sister Holmes, I don't feel a thing about Guy, but I have enough confidence in you that I'll go with you and we will find a place. As I was coming from Kansas a few days ago, I passed through Greenbrier, which is just five miles from Guy, and it's a good size town. Don't you think God would let you go to Greenbrier?"

I said, "Brother Blakley, I know it sounds crazy, but I fear the Lord. When the Lord spoke through me and said 'Go to Guy,' I think He could have said Greenbrier as easy as He could say Guy."

He said, "All right Sister Holmes, to Guy we go." The next day Brother and Sister Blakley and I went to Guy. We stopped at a flea market about a mile from Guy. A couple walked in just ahead of us. The lady told the clerk that she was looking for a certain kind of cup. I told them, "We are looking for a place to have a revival." The lady looking for the cup asked, "What religion are you?" We told her Pentecostal. She asked, "What kind of Pentecost?" We answered Jesus' name. She said, "That's what we are." She told us that they lived about thirty miles away and were not going to church anywhere. I asked if we found a place for services, would they come? She and her husband said, "Sure!"

117

We drove on to Guy, where we noticed an old vacant laundromat. As we drove into the parking lot, we met the owner who was just leaving. We rented the building right then and there.

We began getting things set up for service in the next few days. Brother Blakley began knocking on doors. He called and told me he had invited one lady who said, "I don't guess I'll come. We're Church of Christ, and we don't believe in music." I said, "Brother Blakley, why didn't you tell her we won't have any music because neither you nor I can play anything."

The Lord let everything just fall into place. Brother Blakley went to a store in front of the laundromat to invite a lady who said, "I'll come. Do you have an altar bench?" We had a pulpit and chairs that we had carried from the North Little Rock church. We didn't think we would need an altar the first night, but when she insisted, Brother Blakley took the altar. Sure enough, a man and his wife went to the altar the first service.

Brother Eugene Goodnight in the home church remembered he had stored some church pews from a vacant church that he had bought and converted into a garage. He donated the pews and they fit the old laundromat nicely. Brother Paul Connor ran into such a bargain in sound equipment that he couldn't pass it up. He had bought it not knowing what he would do with it. After visiting the services at Guy, he donated it.

Brother Brent Calvert asked Brother Blakley if he had an organ for Guy. When he said no Brother Calvert said, "You have one now. All it will cost you is a trip to Kansas City to pick it up." Brother Calvert said that he had found such a bargain that he couldn't pass it up. "I bought it," he said, "and didn't know what I'd do with it."

The very first service the Woodes and Beards (the two families that I had visited on my first trip to Guy) were there. Brother Woods brought his bass guitar to play. The Woodes and Sister Beard sang specials. They were the first ones to get baptized in Jesus' name. The couple we met at the flea market were also there the first night. She played a guitar and he played an accordion; so even though Brother Blakley and I didn't play, we never lacked music.

The Lord blessed and the church started to grow. They eventually bought six acres with a house, which was renovated into a small church. Half of the building was the main auditorium and the other half was Sunday school rooms and a small fellowship hall. The monthly payment was $350.

When Brother Blakley was growing up in North Little Rock, his neighbor, Mr. Morgan, was a good friend to him. Before Mr. Morgan died, he told his niece from Tennessee that he wanted Brother Blakley to preach his funeral, which he did. When Mr. Morgan's niece returned to

Guy Church

Tennessee after the funeral, she wrote Brother Blakley a letter, enclosing a check for $350. She wrote, "I feel like sending you this same amount until January of next year." This was in the summer. When January came, she wrote again, "Somehow it seems like I just can't forget about your church at Guy, so I will continue to send the same amount every month." Isn't God wonderful? That was the very amount Brother Blakley needed every month to make the payment on the church and land.

One day a man unknown to Brother Blakley called him on the telephone and said, "The Lord has just spoken to me to give you some money. I'm sending my wife over there with it."

When the lady arrived, she told Brother Blakley, "My husband is drunk, but he said that the Lord spoke to him to give you this." She handed him a one hundred-dollar bill.

After several years, the church began to get crowded. One Sunday night there wasn't even enough room to set out chairs for all the people. Brother Blakley announced, "I feel it's time to expand the auditorium. All the men who can, meet with me in the morning and we'll remove this partition to make the auditorium bigger."

The next morning before anyone else but Brother Blakley had

119

Brother & Sister Blakley and Michael

arrived, a man unknown to Brother Blakley stopped by the church and said, "Preacher, what are you doing?" Brother Blakley explained the expansion project to the man. The next morning the same man stopped by again and said, "Preacher, I don't go to church anywhere, but I do believe in tithing. I've brought you an offering." When Brother Blakley accepted the check, he looked at it and realized it was for $3,500, the very amount that was needed for the current project.

Since the first service, there has been miracle after miracle at Guy. To God be all the glory! Today a beautiful church sits on six acres of land. One of the greatest miracles is the way that God sent Brother and Sister Blakley to Guy to pastor that spiritually hungry group of people. Every need has been met. There is no doubt that God has opened the seal on a fountain and opened a well that was shut up. A spirit of worship is in every service, and God is still working miracles.

Chapter 27

✝

Sheridan, Arkansas

About fifteen years ago, before the Lord ever led me to Guy, I'd be praying and speaking in tongues and the Lord would speak through me in English, "I see a sign, it's a gold sign; I see 'sold' on the sign." I thought we'd find it at Guy but we didn't. Sometimes it would be six months before the Lord would speak those words again.

One day as I was praying, the Lord spoke these words to my heart; "What I've done in Guy I want to do in Sheridan." I was shocked but there was no doubt; I knew it was the Lord.

One day when Faith and I were in Sheridan looking for a building, I said to her, "I have never seen it come to pass what the Lord spoke to me, "I see a sign, it's a gold sign; I see 'sold' on the sign." Another day Janet went with me to look for a place in which to have some services. I thought that maybe the Lord had another vacant laundromat, but it seemed every place was filled. The burden became greater and I went back again and again.

One day when Janet and I were driving around Sheridan, we drove up to a Baptist church with a sign out front. I said, "Janet, what would you call that color? Would it be a gold-like color?" (I'm colorblind.)

She said, "Yes."

I said, "Well, that must be my sign that the Holy Ghost has been speaking about these fifteen years." We called to see what price they wanted for the church and they said $200,000. I thought, "Lord, we could never afford that."

On another visit to Sheridan, we drove in front of the church and I raised my hands and said, "God, just give us this church." I really didn't see how it could happen, but I still asked the Lord. Then we discovered that the church had been sold to a doctor's son. We called his mother and she said she thought he would sell it, but we could never seem to make contact with him. I told Brother Joel, "That church might have to sell again if that's what God wants for us." And sure enough, that's exactly what happened.

Mr. Webb, a man who owned a paper company, bought the church from the doctor's son in the hope that some day it would be a Pentecostal church. His lease had expired on the building he was using and he was going to have to move. He bought this church because it had many large rooms attached to the back behind the Sunday school rooms. There was plenty of space for his business without using the auditorium or the Sunday school rooms.

A man tried to rent the church to use as a flea market, but Brother Webb said no. We learned that he came one morning before dawn and walked around the church praying, "Lord, make a Pentecostal church out of this building."

In the meantime, we had found a vacant storefront to rent for services. Just before we wrote the three hundred-dollar check for the storefront, we heard that the church had sold again. Brother Holmes, my son-in-law Ronnie and I drove down there to meet Brother Webb and ask him what he would rent it for. He said, "Well, I promised it to some Nazarene people who are wanting to rent it. They are supposed to let me know something Monday. You can call me Monday to see if they are going to take it."

He and Brother Holmes were talking in the auditorium of the church. Brother Holmes stepped aside and he started praying and crying and speaking in tongues. He put a fleece before the Lord, "Lord, if this is the place where you are leading us, just don't let them call, and we'll know that you want a church in Sheridan."

After Monday, Brother Webb called Brother Holmes and said, "Those people never did call back so if you want it, you can have the church." He was so happy. He wanted to rent us the building for $35 a month. Brother Holmes told him, "My mother and sister were about to rent a store building just a few streets over, just a small building for $300 a month." Brother Webb replied, "Well, you can have the church for $35 a month." The church probably seats around 500. He said, "You pray. If the Lord would bless my business I would like to contribute the rent to the work of the Lord."

There was another witness that the hand of the Lord was upon that church building. We later found that Brother and Sister Wallingsford had prayed for three years that the vacant building would become a Pentecostal church. They knew nothing about my burden for Sheridan.

The church is beautiful red brick with white trim. It has hardwood floors and plenty of Sunday school rooms. It even has an elevator for someone in a wheel chair, or for someone unable to walk up steps.

Between forty and fifty people from Sheridan attended the first service. We are having service there every Saturday night. Words cannot explain how the presence of the Lord has met with us every service. For years I have carried this heavy burden for Sheridan. Many times the Holy Ghost has spoken through me, "Go, and I will seal them." The way I understand, He seals with the Holy Ghost. We are looking for a great revival in the town of Sheridan.

Janet and I try to go an hour to an hour-and-a-half before service to pray. A few nights ago, Sister Weaver went with us. As we were praying, I was begging the Lord to send revival to Sheridan. And just as clear as could be I heard a voice saying, "Not yet, but I will." I had heard this voice before saying that very thing, but I just couldn't remember where I had heard it. I told Janet and Sister Weaver about it and said, "Help me pray that the Lord will bring this back to my mind, the person that said this."

About a week later I went on a trip with Brother Joel, Sharon and Faith to see one of Brother Holmes's sisters in a nursing home near New Orleans. Brother and Sister Cox were with us and they suggested that we go to New Orleans to eat supper. Right after I walked into the restaurant the Lord revealed to me where I had heard that voice; it was over thirty years ago in New Orleans, where I was preaching a revival for Sister Gatlin. One morning a man called and I answered the telephone. When Sister Gatlin answered on the extension, I realized that this man was very angry and speaking so rudely to her. She said, "I'll pay you tomorrow. I'll bring it to you tomorrow." When she hung up the telephone I asked her what was wrong. She said, "I owe him for a heater".

I said, "Do you have the money to pay him?"

She laughed, "Not now, but I will!"

I said, "You just take the offering up for that tonight."

She said, "I wouldn't do that for anything." She was relaxed about it but it worried me because the man was so upset.

The next morning a sinner man who had been coming to church called and said that he wanted to take Sister Gatlin, Sister Frances Price (who lived with Sister Gatlin) and me out to eat. He said, "When I come, I am going to bring $100 for Sister Gatlin, $100 for Sister Holmes and $100 for Sister Price." Years ago, $100 was a lot of money (like $1,000 would be today). The restaurant was close to the house of the man Sister Gatlin owed, so she left us at the restaurant and went and paid for the heater. The Lord let me know he wasn't able to just pay the bill but even gave an extra blessing to Sister Price and me.

As I was praying and crying for a revival at Sheridan, the Lord let me know that He was going to send it. He also revealed that He would do twice as much at Sheridan as what He has done at Guy, so we are looking for great things at the church in Sheridan.

Now the Lord has blessed and given them a great pastor and his wife, Brother and Sister Parker. You could never find a pastor and wife with any greater burden for lost souls than they have.

Reverend & Sister Parker

Church at Sheridan

Chapter 28

✝

Introduction to "He Keeps Me Singing"

It was some time in the sixties after that I had purposed in my heart to do some extra praying and seeking the Lord that I began to feel the presence of the Lord in a special way. The Lord, I will always feel, just dropped a little handful on purpose for me. I neither know music nor do I have a talent to sing, but the Lord anointed me to write a song I titled "Wade Out."

After this the Lord gave me many songs. Sometimes when I was going through a trial, my soul would be so blessed and uplifted through another new song. I remember Brother Holmes and I were in Kansas City and I was so burdened for one of my loved ones when I wrote the following song:

> I'm not the one that driving; I'm just merely riding.
> My God has His hands upon the wheel.
> He knows each curve and danger; to this road He's no stranger.
> I'm on my way; I'll soon be home.

Before Brother Holmes went to be with the Lord, he told me one day, "Now if the Lord takes me and you are left, don't stop working for the Lord. You keep on preaching revivals."

I'll never forget when I first began traveling alone from one revival to another. I missed him so much, but God was so sweet and real to me. One day as I was driving between Pine Bluff and McGehee on my way to a revival for Brother Larry Murray in Meadville, Mississippi, I began to sing as words came to my mind. "In your presence I behold the beauty of the Lord." And the Lord gave me the song "A Coal of Fire from Off the Altar." The miles seemed so short even though I was traveling alone. Although many years have passed, I still remember some of the very times and the places where I'd be inspired to write a song. I will always remember the Lord giving me words for the songs that follow.

I've Got To Make It On In

(1)   I've come so far down this road of life.
I've met with foe; and I've met with strife;
But I've found my God to be a real, real friend.
By His wonderful grace, I can make it on in.

(Chorus)   I've got to make it on in, Lord,
I've got to make it on in.
I can't turn around,
I'm too near the end.
This cross I bear, I'll trade it for a crown
When I hear Him say, "My child, well done."

(2)   Sometimes it seems that life is unfair,
That nobody knows or seems to care.
When the day is dark and the nights are cold,
I know my God is trailing this road.

Tell God You Love Him

If you're discouraged and filled with fear,
Just call on Jesus; He's always near.
He'll fight your battles and make you strong,
He'll lift your burdens, give you a song

Tell God you love Him; He loves you, too.
His heart is yearning; He'll take you through.
He's always standing with a helping hand
To cross you over to Caanan's land

Remember Moses down in Egypt land;
He led God's people with a mighty hand.
The waters rolled back and stood like a heap
While Israel crossed over with dry feet.

I Miss You, Brother Holmes

Our home is not the same, you see
Where once your voice was speaking, it seems so silently.
When I walk into the room and see the ole' wheel chair,
Then I think of Heaven and I see you walking there.

If only in this life, I'd be most miserable,
But soon I'll step inside the gates.
Will you please watch for me?
The race is not unto the swift,
Nor the battle to the strong.
So by God's love and grace,
We'll all soon be home.

I miss your smile, I miss your prayers,
I miss your tears.
All that's left are memories
Of how we labored together through the years.
I know Heaven has called you now,
So now I'll journey on, and one day
If I'll be faithful, I'll join you around the throne.

GONNA TAKE A VACATION

Gonna take a vacation, gonna leave this fair land,
Go sailing across Jordan and join the heavenly band.
When I walk through that City, His face I shall see.
I'll be taking a vacation for eternity.
It'll be good-bye to trials, good-bye to tears.
Good-bye to sorrow, good-bye to fear.
Hello to Heaven, when I walk through the gate,
Just show me my mansion, I've come here to stay.

I'll put on a robe as white as the light.
I'll wear a crown that's shining so bright.
I'll join with that number on the glassy sea;
I'll be praising my Savior through eternity.

MISSION ACCOMPLISHED

"Mission Accomplished!" that's what I want to say
When I see Jesus just inside the gate.
That's why I'm striving day after day,
"Mission Accomplished!" That's what I want to say.

I hear Paul talking from an old Roman jail
Writing a letter, a message he wanted to tell,
"I've finished my course; may leave just any day;"
"Mission Accomplished!" That's what I heard him say.

From the dusty roads of Bethany to Golgotha's hill,
A heavy cross, a broken heart but yielded to the Father's will.
He said, "It's finished; I'm leaving this body of clay."
"Mission Accomplished!" That's what I heard him say.

It'll Be Worth Every Mile

I've faced some hard battles on life's battlefield.
I've had some hard trials, but through God's grace I'll never yield.
I've seen some great victories for God that have been won,
And thanks to Calvary for the race I have won.

It'll be worth every mile, just wait and you will see.
It'll be worth every hour you've spent down on your knees.
There'll be things to enjoy throughout eternity.
It'll be worth every mile of the trip, just wait and see.

I've crossed many deserts in my life's span.
I've walked through valleys by the touch of His hand.
I've traveled many miles through sunshine and rain,
Not seeking for pleasure or earthly gain.

Oceans of Blessings

Oceans of blessings, rivers of peace,
Streams of pure water falling at my feet.
Enjoying His presence every step I take,
Resting in His shadow in the heat of the day.

I am so happy! I found the pearl of great price.
I just started living when I surrendered my life.
I asked the Master, "Where do you feed your sheep?"
"Down by the shepherd's tent," He answered so sweet.

Into the holiest of holies, in the cleft of the rock,
I found myself hiding from the storms of the night
Listening for His voice, soon to say,
"The harvest is ended, my love, come away."

We're on Our Way

We've traveled many miles together,
Sometimes in stormy weather,
The darkness of the night would be upon.
I hear a small voice whisper,
Be still, my child, and listen.
We're on our way,
We'll soon be home.

I'm not the one that's driving.
I'm just merely riding.
My God has his hand upon the wheel.
He knows each curve and danger;
To this road He's no stranger.
I'm on my way,
I'll soon be home.

Let My Life Be of Service to Thee

Let my life be of service to Thee;
Make my life like a light shinning free.
Help me to tell of Thy sweet love
From the one from up above.
Let my life be of service to Thee.

I'll follow His footsteps all the way;
I'll listen for His voice to obey.
I'll work, work in the fields,
My strength to Him I do yield.
Let my life be of service to Thee.

Make my life a blessing today;
Help me to help someone along the way.
Though my strength may be small,
Yet to Thee, I give my all.
Let my life be of service to Thee.

Chapter 29

The Power of Choice

"If it seem evil unto you to serve the Lord, choose you this day whom you will serve" (Joshua 24:15). God has given unto men the power of choice. The choice we make in this life will determine where we will be a million years from today.

I heard about a minister who, when conducting a funeral service, stepped to the pulpit and spoke these words: "The person who lies here before us today is right now where he chose to be." No doubt the audience thought, "How crude." When you stop to think about it though, it is so true.

> Moses, when he was come to years, refused to be called the son of Pharaoh's daughter; *choosing* rather to suffer affliction with the people of God, than to enjoy the pleasures of sin for a season; esteeming the reproach of Christ greater riches than the treasures in Egypt: for he had respect unto the recompense of the reward (Hebrews 11:24-26).

Had Moses remained in Egypt, he eventually would have sat upon the throne. But because he *chose* the afflictions of the righteous rather than the pleasures of sin, the Lord reserved for Moses the leadership of his own chosen people. This was a much higher office! Even though he faced many trials, he was privileged to experience many miracles. The crossing of the Red Sea, water coming from a dry rock, manna raining from Heaven to feed them, all of their shoes lasting forty years; and furthermore, they enjoyed perfect health, and Moses had an angel for his guide!

Then came his mountaintop experience. What an exciting day it was when the Lord called him to come up to Mt. Sinai. There he saw God face to face and was privileged to receive from Him the Ten Commandments.

Later, after many years of walking in the presence of the Lord, Moses went up from the plains of Moab unto the mountain of Nebo. "So Moses, the servant of the Lord died there in the land of Moab, according to the word of the Lord. And He buried him in a valley in the land of Moab, over against Beth-peor, but no man knoweth of his sepulchre unto this day" (Deuteronomy 34:5, 6). What greater recognition could Moses have received than to be called "a servant of the Lord" and to be buried by the very hand of God Himself?

Had he chosen to stay in Egypt, no doubt the epitaph on his tomb there would have been "Moses, the Adopted Son of Pharaoh's Daughter." Do you think he made the right choice?

The next news we hear of Moses, he's upon another mountain, the Mount of Transfiguration, where he appeared and talked with Jesus, who was transfigured before Peter, James and John. Had Jesus requested Moses to sing a special that day, can't you just hear Moses singing, "I'm not in the valley; I'm just changing mountaintops!"

Let's say it was possible today to be a spectator in one of Heaven's grandstands. You might request that Moses be put on the witness stand where you could ask him, "Moses, did it pay for you to forsake Egypt and suffer the afflictions of the people of God rather than to enjoy the pleasures of Egypt?" We know his answer would be ten thousand times yes!

Can't you see it is important that you make the right choice in this life? When Jesus was visiting in the home of Mary and Martha, Mary sat down at the feet of Jesus listening to his words while Martha was busy with material things. When Martha came to Jesus and desired that He would ask her sister to get up and help her, Jesus said, "Martha, Martha, thou art careful and troubled about many things. Mary has chosen the good part that shall not be taken away from her." If we were to gain the whole world and lose our soul, what would it profit us?

God has a plan, which was preached by the early church, for man to choose to be saved. The Book of Acts is the history of the early church. Jesus told his disciples, "I'm going away, but I'll send you another Comforter." The first chapter of Acts gives the number (120) that returned from Mt. Olivet after watching Jesus ascend into the heavens. Notice, in Acts 2, Mary the Mother of Jesus was present with them. They all received the Holy Ghost and spoke in other tongues as the Spirit gave the utterance. Acting like drunk people, they were making so much noise that a multitude of people gathered.

Some mocked, others doubted and questioned, but then they were under conviction and came to Peter and the rest of the apostles and asked, "Men and brethren, what must we do?"

Peter answered, "Repent and be baptized every one of you in the name of Jesus Christ for the remission of sins, and you shall receive the gift of the Holy Ghost" (Acts 2:38).

Three thousand more received this Bible experience that day. Shortly thereafter, five thousand others believed and received the same experience.

Cornelius sent for Peter because an angel appeared unto him and told him to send for Peter. As Peter preached in Cornelius's house, the Holy Ghost fell on all of them which heard the Word. Some Jews that came with Peter from Joppa said, "We know that they have received the Holy Ghost as well as we because we heard them speaking in tongues" (Acts 10:45,46).

More of John's followers received the Holy Ghost and were baptized (Acts 19:5,6). Why don't you want to repent and be baptized in the lovely name of Jesus, the highest name in Heaven or earth? Think of the greatness of God. He can hold the water of the seas in the palm of his hand, weigh every mountain, speak to hills and they skip like lambs. All power is given unto Him in heaven and earth. He made the moon, sun, and stars, the whole world. In his great wisdom, he has provided the Bible plan for salvation (Matthew 28:18; Acts 2:38; Acts 4:12; Genesis 1:1).

The angels desire to look into this experience. How could anyone be ashamed of something so wonderful as the baptism of the Holy Ghost? It's righteousness, joy, and peace. It's the experience Jesus was telling Nicodemus about (John 3). He told him, that except he was born of the water and Spirit, he couldn't see the kingdom of God. Remember, if you fail to make the right choices, you will be lost and cast into outer darkness to spend an endless eternity.

Chapter 30

✝

Don't Argue with God's Word

Argue with your neighbor, argue with your banker, argue with the IRS;
but please don't try to argue with God's Word because God's Word
means exactly what it says. Eternity is too long, life too uncertain, and
death too sure to take a small chance.

> And in the days of these kings shall the God of heaven set up a king-
> dom, which shall never be destroyed: and the kingdom *shall not be left*
> *to other people*, but it shall break in pieces and consume all these king-
> doms, and it shall stand for ever (Daniel 2:44).

Some may not appreciate this tract and do as King Jehoiakin did
when the Word of the Lord was read unto him. He said, "Bring me a
penknife." Sitting by the hearth, he cut the Word into pieces and cast it
into the fire. But that didn't change God's Word. The Bible is like the
Irishman's fence, which was three feet high and three feet wide; turn it
over or kick it over, and it was still a fence. Although some may scoff at
the Word and ignore it, "Heaven and earth shall pass away, but my Words
shall not pass away" (Matthew 24:35).

God's Word is forever settled, fixed, and unequivocal. The
Scriptures verify that God is very specific and precise in His instructions.
In the very beginning, He told Adam and Eve not to eat of the tree that
was in the midst of the garden. Because they failed to deny their flesh the
forbidden fruit, they lost their home and were driven out of the garden
from the presence of the Lord (Genesis 3).

"Behold, to obey is better than sacrifice" (I Samuel 15:22).

Before Gideon went to battle, God directed him to take his ten thousand soldiers down to the water and to set aside those who lapped water
like a dog, putting their hands to their mouths. The others who bowed

down on their knees and drank were sent back (Judges 7:5, 6).

Naaman was a mighty man of valor, but he had a problem. He had leprosy. The prophet of the Lord told Naaman's servant to tell Naaman to go to Jordan and dip seven times and he would be cured. Naaman argued with his servant. "Why Jordan? Are not Abana and Pharpar, rivers of Damascus, better than all the waters of Israel? May I not wash in them and be clean?" He became very upset. Naaman had another problem besides leprosy: pride. Naaman could have dipped in any other river besides Jordan, but he would never have been healed until he did exactly what God said (II Kings 5).

Many people will not be obedient to God's Word today for the same reason: too much pride. And God hates pride.

Zachariah prophesied, "Thy King cometh, lowly, and riding upon an ass, and upon a colt the foal of an ass" (Zechariah 9:9). Had it been some of us, we would have wanted to ride the finest horse with the finest saddle and all the accessories. And that is what people are doing today riding their proud horses, riding right on off into Hell.

When the angel appeared to Mary giving her the message of the birth of Jesus, although she knew she was going to be misjudged, she said, "Lord, be it unto me according to thy word" (Luke 1:38).

David penned these words: "Thy Word is a lamp unto my feet, and a light unto my path" (Psalm 119:105).

> ... Broad is the way, that leadeth to destruction, and many there be which go in thereat; because strait is the gate, and narrow is the way, which leadeth unto life, and few there be that find it. (Matthew 7:13,14).

When the disciples had fished all night and had caught nothing, Jesus stood on the bank and gave them some instruction. They said, "Master, we have toiled all night and caught nothing. Never the less *at thy* word, we let down the net." When they pulled the net up this time, they couldn't believe the difference.

It is the same way with many today who join the church and attend regularly, but go home just like they went: a few dry songs and a dry sermon. Why don't you just crucify that old proud flesh and say, as did Mary, "Be it unto me according to thy word." Obey the Word of God.

Please read Acts, chapter 2. When the people came to Peter and the rest of the apostles they asked, "Men and brethren, what shall we do?"

Then Peter standing up with the other apostles said, "Repent, and be baptized everyone of you in the name of Jesus Christ for the remission of sins, and ye shall receive the gift of the Holy Ghost."

Mary, the mother of Jesus, had just received the Holy Ghost. Jesus just a few days before had opened the understanding of the apostles and had instructed them just where to go and what to do. They knew that Father and Holy Ghost were titles. Ghost means a spirit, and holy means it was a Holy Spirit. They knew Jesus was the name. That is why in the Scriptures these titles, Father, Son and Holy Ghost, were never used by the apostles when they baptized.

The apostle Paul wrote, "Moses was admonished of God when he was about to make the tabernacle: for, See, saith he, that thou make all things according to the pattern shewed to thee in the mount" (Hebrews 8:5).

Friends, if God was that specific about the natural tabernacle, that even the curtains and all else had to be made according to the pattern he had showed Moses, doesn't that tell us something: that God's Word means what it says, and if we make Heaven, we must go by the pattern? We must cut our lives down to fit the Word and not keep trying to cut the Word to fit our proud *flesh*.

Obedience to the Word is where the real joy and peace are. When we are baptized in his lovely name and receive the infilling of the Holy Ghost, we are so happy and feel no doubt of being ready to meet God. You don't care what the world thinks or says about you!

How could anyone be ashamed to be baptized in the name of Jesus, which is the greatest name in heaven or on earth?

Please take warning. God's pattern for this great salvation is not popular with the world. "... not many wise men after the flesh, not many mighty, not many noble, are called" (I Corinthians 1:26). Notice He didn't say any, but *many*. So this great plan is for everyone. Mark penned these words speaking of Jesus' teaching, "And the common people heard him gladly" (Mark 12:37). Jude wrote, "Beloved, when I gave all diligence to write unto you of the common salvation" (Jude 3).

Friends don't let pride, fame, money, or anything cause you to be lost for eternity. The last thing we hear from the rich man in Hell (Luke chapter 16), he's begging for water and crying that his loved ones not come where he is.

Chapter 31

Saved or Deceived?

Do you believe the Bible is true? A person who doesn't believe the Bible is true and that it means exactly what it says, is already deceived. For Romans 3:4 reads, "God forbid, yea, let God be true, but every man a liar."

Do you believe that just any way you decide to take in this life will lead you to Heaven? Some people do. People like this remind me of an old maid praying the Lord would send her a husband. One day she knelt under a tree. She didn't know that in the branches sat a big hoot owl. When she asked the Lord to please send her a husband, the owl said, "Who, who." She answered, "Just anybody, Lord, anybody."

The Bible says in Ephesians 4:5, "One Lord, One Faith, One Baptism." Not just any way will do. The Bible also says to search the Scriptures for in them ye think ye have eternal life. In other words, some people think they have eternal life according to the Scriptures but they don't. They need to search further. Eternity is too long to take a chance on your soul.

Are you following the strait path? "Because strait is the gate, and narrow is the way, which leadeth unto life, and few there be that find it (Matthew 7:14). When a carpenter is asked, "Is this a straight line?" No doubt he will say, "Check it by the rule." The Bible is our rule. Are you wondering if your path is straight? Check it by the rule.

Do you have signs and wonders in your midst? An error some people make is in feeling that because signs and wonders are in their midst they must be following the rule.

"And many false prophets shall rise, and shall deceive many" (Matthew 24:11).

"For false Christs and false prophets shall rise, and shall show signs and wonders, to seduce, if it were possible, even the elect" (Matthew 24:24). Notice it said *false* prophets will show signs and wonders. Evidently the presence of signs and wonders does not automatically ensure salvation.

If all ways are not true and all prophets are not true, let's take a short look at the difference between true prophets and false prophets to see who is teaching us to follow the rule. Jesus said unto Nicodemus, "You must be born of the water and of the Spirit, or you cannot see the kingdom of God. Marvel not Nicodemus. You must be born again." There are ministers today who stand in the pulpit and preach that you don't have to be baptized and receive the Holy Ghost to be saved. Isn't baptism a type of being born of water and the Holy Ghost a type of being born of the Spirit? Jesus said that we must be born of water and of the Spirit.

Two other Scriptures come to my mind: "Whereunto even baptism doth also now save us" (I Peter 3:21), and "If any man have not the Spirit of Christ, he is none of His" (Romans 8:9).

Does the Bible really mean what it says? Let's take a look at the apostle Peter's experience and see. The apostles said that it's not only important to be baptized, but it's also necessary to be baptized according to the right formula. In Acts 2, one hundred and twenty had just received the Holy Ghost with the evidence of speaking in other tongues when it was noised abroad and the multitudes came looking on. They first thought that the one hundred and twenty were drunk. Peter realized this and stood up with the other eleven apostles, saying unto them, "These men are not drunk as ye suppose . . . " They became pricked in their hearts and asked the apostles, "Men and brethren, what shall we do?" He said unto them, "Repent, and be baptized everyone of you *in the name of Jesus Christ* for the remission of sins, and ye shall receive the gift of the Holy Ghost. For the promise is unto you, and to your children, and to all that are afar off, *even as many as the Lord our God shall call*" (Acts 2:38,39). On that same day more than three thousand souls received that same experience. Would you say that Peter made a mistake when the told them to be baptized in the name of Jesus? Why didn't he tell them to be baptized in the titles Father, Son, and Holy Ghost? Because it had been less than two weeks since the following had taken place:

> Then opened He (Jesus) their understanding, that they might understand the Scriptures, And said unto them, Thus it is written, and thus it behoved Christ to suffer, and to rise from the dead the third day: And that repentance and remission of sins should be preached in His name among all nations, beginning at Jerusalem (Luke 24:45-47).

Notice He pinpointed the name (His name) and the place

(Jerusalem). I once heard of a lady who said she believed that Peter made a mistake when he said to baptize in the name of Jesus. Another man made the remark that the disciples were a bunch of "dumb bunnies" because they never one time followed Matthew 28:19. What is your opinion? Do you think Peter made a mistake when he told the people to be baptized in the name of Jesus? And did all of the disciples make a mistake when they never one time pronounced the titles over a convert? No, they didn't! They knew that "Father" is not a name – it's a title. "Son" is not a name – it's a title. "Holy Ghost" is not a name – it's a title. Matthew 28:19 said " ... baptizing them in the *name* of the Father, Son and Holy Ghost." They knew the name! Jesus had just opened their understanding! Who would you say are the true prophets: The ones that baptize in the name of Jesus or the ones that use no name at all?

The apostle Paul, who wasn't there on the day of Pentecost, also taught baptism in the name of Jesus. When he met believers who knew only the baptism of John, he " ... expounded unto him the way of God more perfectly." (Acts 18:26) (Acts 19:1-6). Talking to some people later he said:

> I marvel that ye are so soon removed from him that called you into the grace of Christ unto another gospel: Which is not another; but there be some that trouble you, and would pervert the gospel of Christ. But though we, or an angel from heaven, preach any other gospel unto you than that which we have preached unto you, let him be accursed. As we said before, so say I now again, If any man preach any other gospel unto you than that ye have received, let him be accursed (Galatians 1:6-9).

If the Bible is the rule, who are the dumb bunnies? Is it Peter and Paul and the rest of the apostles? Or, is it the preacher who preaches that you don't have to be baptized in Jesus' name and receive the Holy Ghost? You decide.

139

Chapter 32

✝

Does God's Word Offend You?

The word "offend" means to displease, to shock, to cause to sin or neglect duty, to cause dislike or anger.

> Many therefore of his disciples, when they had heard, this, said, This is an hard saying; who can hear it? When Jesus knew in himself that his disciples murmured at it, he said unto them, "Doth this offend you?" (John 6:60,61).

David penned these words: "Great peace have they which love *thy law*: and nothing shall offend them" (Psalm 119:165).

About 3:00 a.m. the Lord awakened me and brought to my mind a dream which I had in the seventies, about thirty years ago. In this dream I was standing on the bank of a creek as my cousin, a minister who lived many miles away, was baptizing people. Every time she would start to baptize one, I would call her by name and jump up and down begging her to say, "In Jesus' name." But she ignored my pleading. Not having seen her in years, I thought it strange to have had this dream.

Less than two weeks later, I went to visit my mother, who lived over three hundred miles away. During my visit Mother heard there was sickness in a cousin's family and suggested that we drive out to the country and visit them. We walked into their house to find my minister cousin sitting there. When the dream immediately flashed into my mind, I thought, "Lord, I must tell her this dream." I dreaded to because I knew she didn't believe in Jesus' name baptism, but I feared the Lord. Sitting there I began thinking what could be so bad about being baptized in Jesus' name, the greatest and the only name on earth given among men whereby we must be saved? How could she let this upset her? I got the courage to say, "Last week I dreamed about you." Smiling, she said, "Tell me the dream." When

I did, her countenance changed, and she became very upset. She was offended and said, "You folks think you are the only ones going to Heaven." It made a very unpleasant atmosphere for the remainder of our visit.

I've learned down through the years that the name of Jesus really upsets some people just as it did in Bible days. When the apostles were stopped from preaching and were beaten, they were told they could preach, but not to preach or teach in His name.

Someone made the same remark my cousin had made to a preacher saying, "Jesus' name people believe they are the only ones going to Heaven."

The preacher replied, "No, Sister, we are not sure about all of us."

I agree! We haven't made it to the finishing line yet. But I do know, according to God's word, repentance, water baptism in Jesus' name, and receiving the infilling of the Holy Ghost starts you in the race.

Naaman, when told by the prophet of the Lord that the condition for receiving his healing was to dip in Jordan seven times, was very offended and went into a rage. But when his servant pointed out to him the foolishness of his disobedience, he decided to swallow his pride and go ahead and dip himself in Jordan.

Oh, Friend, if you want to feel good, clean, and like a brand-new person, repent of your sins and get baptized in the lovely name of Jesus, and let Jesus baptize you with the Holy Ghost and fire. Then you will not be concerned about what the world or even your best friends think about you. You will just have a burden for them all to obey God's word.

"According to the grace of God which is given unto me, as a wise masterbuilder, I have laid the foundation, and another buildeth thereon. But let every man take heed how he buildeth thereupon" (I Corinthians 3:10).

The apostle Peter penned these words: " . . . Behold, I lay in Sion a chief corner stone, elect, precious: and he that believeth on Him shall not be confounded. Unto you therefore which believe he is precious: but unto them which be disobedient, the stone which the builders disallowed, the same is made the head of the corner (Remember, the chief corner stone is where the name is), And a stone of stumbling, and a rock of offense, even to them which stumble at the word, being disobedient: whereunto also they were appointed" (I Peter 2:6-8).

Be honest with yourself and with God. When someone talks to you about water baptism in Jesus' name, does it cause your blood pressure to elevate? If it does, you need to give it a serious second thought because eternity is long and judgment sure. When we stand before God to be sentenced for eternity, the Bible will be opened and we will be judged by the words written in the book.

Chapter 33

✝

Rattling Your Cup or
Spinning Your Wheels

The rich man, with so many important things to do, was busy every day rushing here and there. I have a mental picture of him in the finest clothes, stepping out of the door, holding his bank deposit in his hand and then rushing to the bank to make another deposit in his substantial account.

As he walks through the gate, the rich man hears Lazarus rattling a few coins in a cup. There is a vast difference in the lives of the rich man and Lazarus. The days of Lazarus are not so filled with the cares and pleasures of life. He spends his time in prayer and devotion to God, laying up treasures in Heaven. Can't you just see the rich man as he enjoys driving by and looking at his fine cattle? Since a big party is scheduled at his house tonight, he must rush. He takes off so fast he spins his wheels.

That night the lawn is overspread with cars, and the house is filled with friends. A great banquet abounds with meat, drink, and delightful appetizers. Outside the gate, Lazarus is hungry, desiring a few crumbs; but he doesn't complain because he knows one day he'll sit down at the Marriage Supper of the Lamb. He lies there with the dogs licking his sores; but although physically unable to take a step, he is walking with God in the Spirit, thinking about the day that he'll be taking a vacation to that city with streets of pure gold.

Vacations, various sports, and other pleasures bring delight to the rich man's life. No doubt he thought, "How lucky I've been. This magnificent home with all of these beautiful things I've collected through the years is the finest."

But I see him as he walks into the living room one night and sits down in his beautiful velvet chair. On a table near him lies a closed Bible that contains words of eternal life (the plan of salvation). Disregarding it, he watches the midnight show. Suddenly, he feels a severe pain in his chest. Everything begins to turn dark. He loses consciousness of this life and drifts into the darkest night he has ever experienced.

Suddenly, he feels the effects of a very intense heat. Then he hears the screams and cries of millions as they weep, wail, and beg for water. He too begins to cry and scream, "I'm lost! I'm lost and being cast into an eternal Hell!" The black billows of smoke are boiling, and it is so dark he cannot see who any person is. As some gnash upon him with their teeth, he vaguely recognizes familiar voices. The realization that this is forever and ever brings violent trembling, crying, and screaming. Becoming so thirsty, after only a minute, he looks into a far distance and sees a face he remembers, one he had seen back in yonder world. It was Lazarus in the bosom of Abraham.

After the death of the rich man, the Lord spoke to the angels who were standing at attention around the throne. He sent not just one, but several angels to go to the earth and bring Lazarus home. In a flash, they were at the side of Lazarus. As he beheld these glorious shining beings, brighter than the light, they spoke, "Drop your cup. You'll never need it again. Neither will you ever hunger or thirst again. We have come to take you home." Lazarus drew his last breath in this life and they carried him to that city.

No doubt Lazarus said, "Now this is the day I have lived for." Everything became brighter and brighter as the angels carried him up the Milky Way, past the moon, past the stars. Don't you wonder how excited he was when he began to see the light of that city? In my mind I can hear one of the angels say, "Lazarus, you haven't seen anything yet. Just wait until you see Jesus, the gates of pearl, and your mansion. Also, you have a whole new wardrobe waiting, and we have got to tell you that in the crown room, there is a crown that was make especially for you." Just picture the smile on Lazarus's face as the angel continued, "You are invited to the Marriage Supper of the Lamb. Abraham, Isaac, and Jacob are coming from the East and from the West to sit down at the table where Jesus Christ will gird himself and serve you."

In the midst of the city there is a River of Life, clear as crystal, with fruit trees on both sides. I can hear Lazarus say, "I'm so glad that back in yonder world I stood for Jesus and let the world go by. Now, I'll be a multimillionaire for eternity. Hey Angels, this is what I call really living!"

We can think of only a tiny sample of what Lazarus is enjoying this very hour. "But as it is written, Eye hath not seen, nor ear heard, neither hath it entered into the heart of man, the things which God hath prepared for them that love him" (I Corinthians 2:9).

Let's go back to the rich man. He's the beggar now. Just listen, "Father Abraham, send Lazarus and let him dip his finger in water and cool my parching tongue!" God said, "No. Remember in the other world, thou receiveth good things and Lazarus received evil. Now he's comforted, and you are tormented. Besides this, there is a great gulf fixed between you and him. You can't go where he is, and he can't come to where you are."

Then the rich man remembered his loved ones back in this world and wanted the Lord to send someone to tell them not to come to Hell. (In this life he was no doubt able to run the show, but now God's running things.)

The Lord said, "They have Moses and the prophets. If they won't hear them, they wouldn't hear someone who rose from the dead."

Now, it is not required of you to be a beggar to make Heaven. I admire people who will work and study and achieve goals in this life. But if pride keeps you from being baptized in the precious name of Jesus and receiving the infilling of the Holy Ghost with the evidence of speaking in other tongues according to Acts 2:38, and if you are afraid that this Bible experience would mar your career, I fear for your soul and where you will spend eternity. The apostle Paul said, "But what things were gain to me, those I counted loss for Christ" (Philippians 3:7).

As sure as there is a Heaven, there is a Hell. If you die in your sins, where God is, you can't go. I write this with a burdened heart and compassion for the souls of men.

Please don't go to Hell.

Chapter 34

Something for Yourself

Matthew 6:20

"But lay up for yourselves treasures in heaven, where neither moth nor rust doth corrupt, and where thieves do not break through nor steal" (Matthew 6:20).

Are you interested today in something for yourself? Of course you are. When your friends or loved ones give you something that is personal, there is something about it that gives you a special thrill.

Matthew said, "Laying up for yourselves treasure in heaven." Notice Luke 12:16 speaks of a parable of a certain rich man whose ground brought forth plenty. He was perplexed because there wasn't enough room to bestow all the fruit. He said, "This will I do: I'll tear my old barns down and build new ones in which to bestow all my fruit and goods. I'll say to my soul, 'Take thine ease; eat, drink, and be merry'." But he didn't realize that the death angel would call at his house that night.

The Lord said, "Thou fool, this night thy soul shall be required of thee, and whose shall those things be which thou hast provided?" This man hadn't really done anything for himself.

My soul is stirred when I see people laboring so hard in the hot sun until their hands are full of corns and calluses, but go on neglecting their soul salvation, the most important thing in this world.

In Luke the sixteenth chapter we read of another man leaving this world a pauper. Even though he was rich in this life, he failed to do anything for himself. He must have fought for life, as the vulture of death yawned with indifference and swallowed him. He had lived in the walls of neglect and selfishness, and now the walls of hell surrounded him. Can't you just see the hungry flames of hell fencing him in? Here he found time to pray. But did he pray for gold? Did he pray to see his marble walls, or his fields of smiling harvest, or to recline on his couch of luxury? No, he prayed for water, a drop of water. Had he taken time to pray in this life, he could have enjoyed drinking from the River of Life that John saw while he was in exile on the Isle of Patmos.

Notice the rich man's prayer wasn't answered.

The purpose of this article is to stir you up to lay up something for yourself. Our lives here are such a short span. Many people live for the day when they can retire and take life a little easy, but it seems that in so many cases the death angel is right down the next block moving their way.

The Apostle Paul wrote to Timothy from Rome when the sentence of death had been passed upon him. "For I am now ready to be offered, and the time of my departure is at hand. I have fought a good fight. I have finished my course; I have kept the faith: Henceforth there is laid up *for me a crown of righteousness*, which the Lord, the righteous Judge, shall give *me* at that day; and not to me only, but unto all them also that love His appearing."

So Friend, repent today and be baptized in the name of Jesus Christ for the remission of sins and receive the Holy Ghost with the evidence of speaking in other tongues as the Spirit gives utterance according to the Scripture Acts 2:38. Then live a Spirit-filled life and you will be rich throughout eternity.

Chapter 35

Are You Ashamed of the Gospel?

"There was a man of the Pharisees, named Nicodemus, a ruler of the Jews. The same came to Jesus by night . . ." (John 3:1, 2). Could it have been his prominence and position which brought Nicodemus by night? Do you suppose he was ashamed to be seen talking to the Lord? How could anyone be ashamed of this great Bible salvation for which Jesus paid such a price on the cross at Calvary, that we can be saved? A God with such wisdom who made a world so beautiful; dotted the sky with stars; carpeted the hills, valleys and mountain sides with a carpet of green grass, tiny blue daisies, and other colorful flowers. Millions of beautiful things He has made for us to enjoy, but the greatest thing God has provided for mankind is the baptism of the Holy Ghost.

It's something the angels have desired to look into (I Peter 1:12). It's Christ in us, the hope of glory (Colossians 1:27). Jesus said, "I'm with you but I shall be in you" (John 14:17). It's a comforter (St. John 14:26). It's *righteousness, peace and joy* (Romans 14:17). It's a seal, saith the Scriptures, whereby you are sealed unto the day of redemption (Ephesians 4:30). A seal marks a finished transaction. It's being born again of the Spirit. Jesus was telling Nicodemus he could never see Heaven except he was born of the water and the Spirit (St. John 3:3). It's the infilling of the Holy Ghost, which was experienced by the one hundred twenty, including the apostles and Mary, the mother of Jesus, on the day of Pentecost (Acts 2:4). They all spoke in tongues as the Spirit gave the utterance which is the evidence of having received the Holy Ghost. Now how can anyone let Satan cause him to be ashamed to receive this wonderful Bible experience when Jesus purchased it with His blood on the cross at Calvary?

Let us look at the life of the apostle Paul. Before he received the Holy Ghost, he hated this Bible truth. He held the coats of the mob while they stoned Stephen to death (Acts 7:59). After this we see his intensified fighting of truth. He made havoc of the church.

> And Saul, yet breathing out threatenings and slaughter against the disciples of the Lord, went unto the high priest, and desired of him letters to Damascus to the synagogues that if he found any of this way, whether they were men or women, he might bring them bound unto Jerusalem (Acts 9:1, 2).

While on his way as he came near Damascus, a light shone from Heaven brighter than the sun. He fell to the ground and heard a voice saying, "Saul, Saul, why persecutest thou me?" (Notice when he was persecuting God's people, he was persecuting the Lord.) "As ye have done it unto one of the least of these my brethren, ye have done it unto me" (Matthew 25:40).

Paul said, "Who are thou, Lord?" He said, "I am Jesus whom thou persecutest."

Jesus told him to go on down to Damascus where it would be told him what to do. Notice: He never told Paul to go on down to Damascus and join the First Church. There is no Scripture in the Bible where anyone ever joined any church.

The Lord said, "Arise, go unto the city and it shall be told thee what thou must do." The Lord showed Ananias to arise and go into the street called Straight to the house of Judas and inquire for one called Saul, for he is praying and has already seen a vision of your coming and praying for him.

Ananias walked in, and putting his hands on Paul, said, "Brother Saul, the Lord, even Jesus, that appeared to thee in the way as you came, hath sent me that thou mightest receive thy sight and be filled with the Holy Ghost." Paul received his sight, was filled with the Holy Ghost and was baptized.

In my mind I can just imagine the high priest and others back in Jerusalem looking every day for Paul to come back bringing saints of God to be tortured and killed for the name of Jesus. No doubt they were saying, "Wonder what's become of Paul?"

News gets around pretty fast. I'm sure it wasn't long before they heard that Paul was now a disciple of Jesus (a Holy Roller, he might be called today). He became one of them, against whom he had "breathed out threatenings and slaughter." Now he's a preacher. Before Saul left Damascus some of his former friends were trying to kill him.

Paul lost all his popularity with the chief priests and religious friends of the world. After he was filled with the Holy Ghost and baptized in Jesus' name, we know Paul spoke in tongues. He said, "I thank God I speak with tongues more than ye all" (I Corinthians 14:18). "Wherefore, brethren, covet to prophesy, and forbid not to speak with tongues" (I Corinthians 14:39). He preached baptism in the name of Jesus. He met some of John's disciples, whom he baptized in the name of Jesus although John had previously baptized them (Acts 19:1-6).

It didn't take Paul long to realize this gospel is persecuted by the religious world. Paul wrote to the Corinthian Church "Being defamed, we entreat (defamed means disgraced reputation harmed by slander; to entreat means to intercede with God). We are made as the filth of the world, and are the offscouring of all things unto this day" (I Corinthians 4:13).

Paul said, "I write not these things to shame you, but as my beloved sons I warn you" (verse 14). The apostle Paul was trying to prepare all of them for the persecution which would come for this great truth. Paul was not only mocked and laughed at, but he was beaten, thrown into jail, put out of the synagogue, stoned, and left for dead.

Paul was hated for writing such letters as the one to the Galatians. "I marvel that ye are so soon removed from Him that called you into the grace of Christ unto another gospel! Which is not another, but there be some that trouble you, and would pervert the gospel of Christ. But though we or an angel from heaven, preach any other gospel unto you than that which we have preached unto you, let him be accursed. As we said before, so say I now again, if any man preach any other gospel unto you than that you have received, let him be accursed" (Galatians 1:6).

In Romans 1:16, the apostle Paul penned these words: "For I am not ashamed of the gospel of Christ: for it is the power of God unto salvation unto every one that believeth; to the Jew first, and also the Greek." Ashamed means to be put to shame, feeling shame, humiliated. Let us never be ashamed of this great salvation. May we adorn this doctrine so that when Jesus returns for His Church, He won't look at us and bow His head in shame. But we'll hear Him say "Well done, thou good and faithful servant. Enter into the joys of the Lord."

149

Chapter 36

Babylonian Garments

One morning in January, 1998, I was awakened suddenly by these words: "Split skirts are Babylon garments." I was shocked. I had never had such a thought, and I had never heard such an expression.

In a flash came Matthew 13:44, in which the Holy Ghost is compared with a treasure hid in a field. When a man found the treasure, he sold all he had and bought the field. Holy living, including holy dress, is in this field; they are part of this treasure above all treasures. (Satan, our enemy, hates holiness.) The thought came that if saints are not humble enough to be separate from the world, they will not make it. They will lose this treasure.

I reached for my Bible and began to tremble in the fear of God as I read the sad story of Achan's trespass in taking the accursed thing (a Babylon garment, silver and gold). Israel could not stand before her enemies until the accursed thing was removed from the camp. Achan paid for his transgression with his life; and not only his life, but also the lives of his sons and daughters. All that he had was stoned and then burned (Joshua 7).

Then came the words in Judges 7: "And the Lord said unto Gideon, The people are yet too many; bring them down unto the water, and I will try them for thee there: and it shall be, that of whom I say unto thee, This shall go with thee, the same shall go with thee; and of whomsoever I say unto thee, This shall not go with thee, the same shall not go."

Gideon took the ten thousand men to the water where they all drank. The Lord chose the three hundred who stood and lapped, putting their hand to their mouth. Realizing that they were facing an enemy, they were alert and watchful, and they quickly drank just enough to satisfy their need. They focused on the battle at hand.

All were in the army. All drank. But those who were committed, alert, and focused were qualified to be chosen and used by God. And so, saints today face temptations and dangers (some seemingly harmless, but concealing trends which lead far from God's blessings, even to destruction).

When Moses asked Pharaoh to let him lead the Israelites out of Egypt to serve the Lord, Pharaoh countered with a compromise, "I will let you go sacrifice to your God; only do not go very far." Moses refused because he knew the Promised Land of Canaan was flowing with milk and honey. "We are going all the way," he said. Had Moses compromised with Pharaoh, Israel would have gone only a short way. They would have been bound; they would have had no freedom of worship.

Going not far from Egypt, not really leaving, is a type of failing to "abstain from fleshly lusts which war against the soul (I Peter 2:11)." The grace of God teaches to deny ungodliness and worldly lusts and to live soberly, righteously, and godly in this present world (Titus 2:12). Just as a compromise with Pharaoh would have left God's people bound, compromise with the world will leave us bound in the Spirit, without the liberty and the *anointing* of the Holy Ghost

Our Canaan is where the fullness of joy is flowing, rivers of joy springing up unto everlasting life. The anointing of God upon our lives, not drunk with wine wherein is excess, but filled with the Spirit. Speaking to yourselves in psalms and hymns, singing and making melody in your hearts unto the Lord; praying in the Holy Ghost, speaking in tongues, singing in tongues, dancing in the Spirit. Travailing for lost souls. Having in your hearts the peace of God that passes all understanding. Looking for the soon coming of Jesus, the Bridegroom. God's anointing upon our lives.

Let's watch. Let's guard our treasure. Let's be quick to hear. Let's be ready!

Shortly after the Holy Ghost stirred me with these thoughts and I testified about it in church, someone called to my attention a message preached by Brother Phil White, March 13, 1998, in Kansas City, Missouri: "The Second Exodus" (the exodus from Babylon back to Jerusalem). Babylon is a type of a backslidden life. Brother White, among other things, linked split skirts with Babylonian living — a witness of what the Holy Ghost spoke to me.

151

Chapter 37

✝

A Trip Beyond Imagination

"I haven't noticed an air force or army base; no soldiers dressed in uniform."

The guide explained, "There is never any war here."

"This place is so unusual, so bright and beautiful, but I have seen neither sun nor moon, nor power plant to give all this brilliance of light."

"Let me tell you about the light system in this city. It's Jesus," explained the guide. "He is so great, so mighty, so powerful; from His body and His presence flow all this light and glory that you see. This city is fifteen hundred miles square but without one dark spot."

"I'm sure you have noticed there's no night here. Since everyone has a new body that never gets tired, we need no sleep here."

"What about these beautiful roses, and what's this shining beneath these bushes on the ground?"

"That's easy to explain," he said, "When the petals from these roses fall, they turn to pure gold by the time they touch the ground. You must see the acorn trees. When the acorns fall, they turn to precious diamonds!"

"This is such an incredible place. I've never been in a place that there have been so many beautiful things to behold. I've toured this City for days, and each day, I have to say, the sights have exceeded far beyond my imagination."

"Where are the working people? Men riding in trucks and in vans, their faces covered with grit and grime – their callused hands holding lunch pails."

"Oh, no one toils in this land."

"I've searched for hours trying to find where the middle class and really poor people live."

"This may be hard to believe; in fact, what I tell you may almost blow your mind. I'm happy to tell you there are no poor people here. Everybody owns a mansion and is a Holy Ghost millionaire."

"My, this place is so exciting. Looks like everyone would get prepared to come here. When I walked through the gates of pearl, this flowing white robe was handed me and a crown was placed upon my head!"

"Follow me. Now I'll show you your mansion," an angel whispered in a low sweet voice. "You are here to stay. All these treasures and pleasures will never come to an end."

I asked, "Where are the hospitals?"

He said, "You remember John the Revelator said, 'The leaves on the trees are for the healing of the nations'."

"What about the cemeteries? I've not seen a tombstone or cemetery. Where do they bury their dead?"

With a big smile on his face, he said, "No one dies in this land!"

"Another thing that amazes me so greatly is this beautiful river as clear as crystal and all these little children romping and playing, picking up shining pebbles from the bottom. They look like diamonds and pearls."

He assured me, "There is no danger in this river. This water won't drown you."

"I've enjoyed seeing so many young people; in fact, I haven't seen the first old person anywhere."

He said, "Everyone is young here."

"I stood and watched happy people sailing in spectacular sail boats with different colored sails made of pure silk and covered with gold bows of ribbon. All the people wore crowns of gold and flowing white robes as white as the light."

"Help yourself to the fruit on these fruit trees up and down the banks of the river," invited the guide. "Fruit is always there."

"I happened to notice when I pulled a peach from the tree, another peach appeared in its place."

He said, "You are right and you will never have to worry about a faulty piece of fruit, for there are no insects in this land. And if juice falls on your robe, don't worry—this fruit doesn't stain."

I laughed and said, "This has got to be Heaven. I feel so good all the time—no headaches, no back problems. There is no pain"

"Have you noticed what good deep breaths you take?"

"Yes," I replied, "I've noticed that and also that the air seems so pure and clean."

He said, "There is no pollution here."

"I've noticed it's spring time all the time. Everything is so green. I used to read about John, the Revelator's vision, but I never realized it would be like this. I love having angels and saints for neighbors. See all these angels strolling up and down the streets and all these different choirs singing with music so sweet. I notice they keep perfect time. I've never heard one miss a single note or miss one beat. Everyone I meet is smiling and happy. Not one tear have I seen falling down one cheek. I haven't heard a siren blowing or seen an ambulance rushing down the street. I've decided there's never a wreck or an accident on these golden streets."

"No, it's worshipping the Savior, falling down at His feet, giving praise and honor to the One who prepared this place called Heaven, where you don't ever have to feel rushed or worried about anything."

I said, "In this place, every day must be Sunday."

He said, "Better than that; every day is a holiday!"

Chapter 38

✝

The Lord's House

During prayer meeting at the church one morning I began to think of the Scripture: "My house shall be called a house of prayer." Then thoughts began to be quickened to me like this: when you look, you only see pews and church furniture, but this house is stocked to the ceiling with supplies, no matter what the need may be. If it is a car, there is a car lot here; if someone needs tires, new tires are stacked beyond numbers. Even houses (a real estate business) are here. Shoes, clothes, groceries to no end! Miracles are in His stock!

If you are having family problems, you will find the benefit of the greatest and best marriage counselor. If you are having trouble in controlling your temper, speaking unkind words, backbiting; if you are troubled with a spirit of criticism, with a spirit of jealousy, in His house you can be set free!

He is everything you need. He is the great physician. He has a divine healing business that he purchased before he went to Calvary by stripes he suffered on His back. We know that everything we need is in His house, for He said, "Seek ye first the kingdom of God and his righteousness; and all these things shall be added unto you."

David said, "Delight thyself also in the Lord; and He shall give thee the desires of thine heart" (Psalm 37:4). We know the meaning of delight—extremely satisfied. We will not be tempted to rush from his presence when the Holy Ghost is making intercession if we are delighted in Him. They that wait upon the Lord shall renew their strength; they shall run and not be weary, they shall walk and not faint.

In His presence there is fullness of joy; and at His right hand, pleasures forever more.

Chapter 39

✝

The Lord Goes before Us

Near my seventieth birthday, I began noticing people saying, "Watch your step," and reaching out to assist me in getting out of the car or in walking down steps. I hardly knew what to think at first.

One day I drove to Biloxi to preach a revival for Brother Springer. I always stayed in the home of Brother and Sister Springer and loved every minute of it. Sister Betty Springer was always so kind and sweet to me and I was always thrilled to be with them. This time Sister Betty said, "Sister Holmes, don't ever come down here by yourself again. I don't care if you bring two or three with you." I thought, "Sister Springer, you are one of the kindest persons; it would not be that way in every place I could go. Not everyone would appreciate my bringing two of three more for someone to cook for."

Near the closing of the revival, Sister Springer said, "When you start back to Little Rock, you have got to promise me you will stop at Sister Holland's and rest awhile." Sister Holland lived near Jackson. I thought, "What is happening to me?" I kept noticing when I'd look in the mirror I'd see more wrinkles, but I felt so good in my soul and body that surely I could not be getting old.

The revival with the Springer's closed. I'll never forget the morning I had planned to leave for Little Rock. I awoke to find it storming outside.

Sis. Holmes preaching at #1 Fifty-second Place

156

Sister Springer said, "Sister Holmes, Brother Springer and Paul (their son) have had a call to help with a funeral in Laurel so Paul will drive your car to Hattiesburg." I was so thankful. It rained heavily every mile, and there were dark clouds. I thought, "Lord, you are so good to me." When we came to the highway where they had to turn for Laurel, I thanked them and continued the trip alone. Before I got through Hattiesburg, the sun began to shine and there was no more rain all the way to Little Rock.

A few more years passed. Just before camp meeting one year, Sister Janet Ables, a young lady who lived fifty miles away, had started attending our church. I heard someone say that Janet was taking her vacation during camp meeting. I asked her one night if she would like to stay with me during camp meeting so that she would not have to drive so far. She accepted my invitation. I was living alone and later I said to her, "Janet you ought to get a job here in town and live with me." After she went back home, she gave her boss her notice and moved to Little Rock. For awhile, she and I went on revivals, working for the Lord.

One evening after a trip to the grocery store, we drove into the garage and Janet said, "You go on in; I'll bring in the groceries."

I said, "I'll take this bag." On the way in, I decided to play a little trick. I thought to myself, "Young people feel like old people are rather senile." In this bag were two packages of bathroom tissue. When I got to the refrigerator, I crammed one package of the tissue into it and closed the door. I walked a few steps away to hear what she would have to say. When Janet starting unpacking the groceries, she noticed there was only one package of bathroom tissue. She exclaimed, "I know that we bought two four-roll packages of tissue paper. It must have been left out of the bag." She asked me, "Have you put away any groceries?"

I replied, "I have not put anything in the bathroom."

When she put the first thing into the refrigerator, she didn't notice the tissue, but the next time she did. She exclaimed, "Oh, Sister Holmes, I'm losing my mind. I have put bathroom tissue in the refrigerator!" About that time the telephone rang so she ran into the bedroom and answered. It was Sharon, my daughter, calling. Janet said, "Sharon, I'm losing my mind, I have put tissue in the refrigerator."

I thought, "I'll just let you think for a while that you were the one." When I had stood waiting to hear what her reaction would be when she discovered the tissue in the refrigerator, I had hardly been able to keep my face straight. But when she accepted the blame, I laughed and laughed. About midnight I said, "Janet, I'm the one who put the tissue in the refrigerator." We have had a lot of fun together.

Janet has been a blessing to me as well as to the church. We have gone many places together. We flew with Brother and Sister Holmes to the P.S.R. meeting in Fresno, California, and also with a church group to the Holy Land. She works in the office at the church, but she is still like my right hand. The Scripture says that the Lord goes before us and that Scripture has certainly been fulfilled in my life.

Now I'm eighty-one years old. It's been a good life living for the Lord.

Janet Ables